Sexual Satisfaction Secrets to
Beat Erectile Dysfunction

IT'S HARD!

S. SEQUOIA STAFFORD ECTE, MH

IT'S HARD
Sexual Satisfaction Secrets to Beat Erectile Dysfunction

Difference Press, Washington, D.C., USA
© S. Sequoia Stafford, 2020

ISBN: 978-1-68309-265-0

Cover Design: Jennifer Stimson
Editor: Cory Hott
Author Photo Credit: Peter Wodarczyk (www.peterwfotos.com)

DIFFERENCE
P R E S S

ADVANCE PRAISE

"My friend Sequoia Stafford is a modern medicine woman who explores the Great Mystery of sex and intimacy through Tantra, revealing that the most precious and sacred moment of a person's day may be to have an orgasm witnessed by another. This book may guide you to your own personal heart castle held in the arms of your beloved, and if so, she has created very good medicine indeed."

~ Hank Wesselman PhD., anthropologist and author of *The Bowl of Light: Ancestral Wisdom from a Hawaiian Shaman, The Re-Enchantment: A Shamanic Path to a life of Wonder,* and *The Spiritwalker Trilogy.* ~

"What a gift this book is to men and the partners that love them. Sequoia has a way of making you feel at home and at ease with a difficult topic men don't usually want to talk about with a woman. Her down to earth yet sexy style kept me engaged page after page. She makes the journey to S.E.X. M.A.G.I.C. exciting, heartwarming, and eye opening. Get this book and keep it by your bedside along with bottle of warm coconut oil. You'll be ecstatic that you did."

"*It's Hard* is a step by step instruction manual to the ultimate orgasm. Sequoia teaches us that the greatest levels of physical pleasure are found when we journey into the deepest levels of intimacy. The love and candor with which she shares her vast knowledge makes *It's Hard* a must read for every man and woman who seeks a deeper connection in the bedroom and beyond."

"I have known Sequoia for several years. Over those years, my love for her personally and appreciation for the work she does as a healer have grown dramatically. We have spent many hours discussing both philosophical and practical aspects of healing, through which I witnessed her dedication to constant improvement and her passion to share her gifts with others. I am overjoyed that Sequoia has put her insights and best practices in print, providing the context and exercises for self-healing as well as the potential motivation and sense of safety and comfort for people to choose to work with her directly. In either case, you won't be disappointed. "

"Sequoia's book is a deeply moving instructional guide to healing. Part autobiographical, part spiritual guide and part intimate instruction manual, her book is done with loving honesty and with the wish that it will provide sexual health and enjoyment for both men and women."

~ J. King, Silicon Valley, CA ~

For the loves of my life, that have loved me exactly the way I am and exactly the way I'm not. You are a bouquet of roses that give my life awe, purpose and pleasure. I cherish you all and I'm humbled by your unconditional acceptance and love.

All the world's a stage,
And all the men and women merely players;
They have their exits and their entrances,
And one man in his time plays many parts,
His acts being seven ages. At first the infant,
Mewling and puking in the nurse's arms;
And then the whining schoolboy, with his satchel
And shining morning face, creeping like snail
Unwillingly to school. And then the lover,
Sighing like furnace, with a woeful ballad
Made to his mistress' eyebrow. Then a soldier,
Full of strange oaths, and bearded like the pard,
Jealous in honor, sudden and quick in quarrel,
Seeking the bubble reputation
Even in the cannon's mouth. And then the justice,
In fair round belly with good capon lined,
With eyes severe and beard of formal cut,
Full of wise saws and modern instances;
And so he plays his part. The sixth age shifts
Into the lean and slippered pantaloon,
With spectacles on nose and pouch on side;
His youthful hose, well saved, a world too wide
For his shrunk shank; and his big manly voice,
Turning again toward childish treble, pipes
And whistles in his sound. Last scene of all,
That ends this strange eventful history,
Is second childishness and mere oblivion,
Sans teeth, sans eyes, sans taste, sans everything.

~ William Shakespeare, *As You Like It* ~

TABLE OF CONTENTS

IMPORTANT VOCABULARY TERMS

I will be using the term lingam when referring to your male sex organs, and when I refer to a woman's sex organs, I will use yoni. Both words show reverence for the magic these two sacred creative areas make together. May you come to enjoy the use of these words as freely as I do.

- **S.E.X. Sacred Experience of Xstasy** is a term you will see throughout the book to express the concept of transforming our relationship to sex from friction-based slapping of skin bags to sacred acts of knowing another person while giving the gift of xstasy.

- **M.A.G.I.C.** is the acronym for the tantra massage process I teach in this book to bring life and engorgement to your erection.

- "**Lingam** (Sanskrit for "shaft of light") is the term for the Hindu god Shiva as represented by a phallus (erect male organ). Usually found in conjunction with the Yoni ("sacred space," woman's vulva) which represents the goddess Shakti – the source of Creative Energy. They conjoin to form Bhrama – the Universe. This is the Hindu Trilogy: the representation of the twins of

Creation and Destruction as the highest manifestations or aspects of the One (Bhrama)." (Urban Dictionary)

- "**Erectile dysfunction** (ED) is defined as the consistent or recurrent inability of a man to attain and/or maintain a penile erection sufficient for sexual activity." (2nd International Consultation on Sexual Dysfunction-Paris, June 28th-July 1st, 2003)

- "The noun **impotence** comes from the Latin *impotentia,* meaning "lack of control or power." Though its most common definition is "the condition of not being physically able to have sexual intercourse," *impotence* can be any kind of physical weakness or ineffectiveness. You might present a very unconvincing argument. The impotence of your message may lead to not a single person agreeing with you." (Vocabulary.com)

Chapter 1

STAGES OF MAN'S ERECTION

When you were a little boy, the way your body functioned fascinated you. It did all these surprising things automatically. It functioned seemingly all on its own. When you were touched, it felt good and those good sensations appeared magical.

The body is magical. One of the most magical areas of the body, I'm sure you would agree, are your genitals and reproductive organs. If you are anything like me, you have been fascinated by how a simple thing like air or a breeze can elicit a shiver of pleasure up your body. That is the magic you will learn about in this book.

I bet you remember one of the first times you felt your lingam get hard. It was a magic that became an obsession. Every chance you got you wanted to play with this new magic to see just what it could do. You even found yourself daydreaming and playing with this magic almost as if you were in a trance.

The body taught you about the automatic response to touch, turn-on, and arousal. I'm sure you remember that it even happened automatically when you didn't want it to happen, and all the ways you came up with to make sure that never happened again.

When I was in my twenties, my boyfriend at the time told me that he would imagine his mom playing video games to make an erection go away. You came up with lots of ways like this to make this magical hard appendage grow and get bigger and then you taught yourself how to control it so it didn't get you in trouble at home, at school, at work, at gym, at the movies, on a first date, et cetera.

The magic of your lingam inspired you to do amazing things in your life. And just like the Shakespeare poem says, you have many stages in life as a man that you go through. You will see how this magic is still available to you in all the stages and how the stages affect the automatic response to get hard and aroused.

Let me say before I get into anything else that I got you. You are in the best of hands no matter what the specifics are of your situation. If you are reading this book, you have probably come here for the hardest of hard conversations.

My specialty is creating a space where anyone can say and ask me anything. With the topic that this book covers and the number of conversations I have had to get to the point where I wrote a book about it, you must know that anything you find in this book will hold what you are dealing with in the most honored, respected, safe, discreet, and supportive way. This is what you can count on with me every time.

Here we are together to get you from painful hard work climaxing to yummy, hard, pleasurable explosions of bliss beyond your wildest dreams. After working with hundreds of men and women who have had intimacy challenges, I've seen and heard what happens when these issues don't get resolved. My heart literally aches for what you are going through because I've been there, it was hard for me too.

You are most likely frustrated by the functionality of your erection. At some point in your sex life you probably had a best ever erection that led to an amazing orgasm and release that you want to get back to.

You are probably not sure if this is the new normal for your sex life and are looking for help to get your sex life to a place where it is easy, simple, and pleasurable without contraptions, procedures, or hard work. You might even be thinking, *Why can't I be hard like those guys in the videos I've seen stay hard for hours?*

I'm guessing that your worst nightmare has somehow crept into your life. I bet you feel all alone in what you are experiencing. You have probably had your attention on your erection since you were a little boy and never had anyone to talk to about it who made it safe to share openly what you are thinking, feeling, and questioning. You are probably beside yourself to fix it and never experience this pain again.

Just when you are getting to an age where you are feeling free to express your sexuality freely and getting to the sweet spot in life when you're looking to reap the rewards of your life's hard work it seems there is more hard work to come. And now you're starting to have issues where you're not sure if you can trust your erection to do its job... hmmm. That must really kill you inside.

You're probably really frustrated but doing your best not to let the rest of your life be affected by this frustration, so you've pushed all the thoughts and feelings about your erection into a box, put the lid on it, and stuffed it away, hoping it would just go away.

Or you've been avoiding that from happening most days, feeling lucky when your lingam worked but not sure, and praying that when the most important opportunity comes along your best pal between your legs will get the job done in superhero style.

Unfortunately, the more you avoid arousal the more your body seems to forget how to do it automatically and it has become hard and something you have to work at. This is frustrating and doesn't feel fair at all.

The reality is that you are not alone. I know that sounds like a cliché, but it's true. This is actually something that a majority of men deal with, but can't talk about it openly for fear of being seen as less than a man. Everywhere I go, when I talk to people about what I do and my work, people open up to me and share that they are dealing with this issue; if they aren't, then they know of someone who is. It is pervasive.

What might also surprise you is that women go through a version of this, too, but because we don't have a lingam, it isn't as obvious. Sadly, I have found that this issue you find yourself in is in all cultures and peoples around the world.

You may be saying, "Is that really true? Are others really struggling as much as me? Do other men, and even women, have thoughts about their sexual parts doing the job they are supposed to do?"

Yep, they do. You will see throughout this book that where you have found yourself is totally normal. It is totally normal to feel like you are the only abnormal one and that you will be the only one who doesn't find a solution. I'm guessing you've had that thought a few hundred million times – the one that says this is never going to change and I'm screwed without solution.

I've been there many times. I bet if you wrote down all the thoughts you have had about your erection, you will find that the majority of them are hard on you. You probably talk – if you really listen – to yourself and your body in ways that you would never let anyone else talk to you. There are real issues you face, like having to talk about this with someone when all you want to do is Do It. Instead you have to look into the eyes of your lover and admit this is hard for you and it sucks, feeling emotions that no one wants to feel, and making choices of how to handle all the aspects of this challenge. I'm going to say this again and again: every sexual being wonders if the magical mystery of pleasure and orgasm will work this time.

Whether you have been dealing with erectile dysfunction for a week or for years, there are hurdles we will be getting over together. I know right now it seems hard, so hard that nothing looks like it will turn this thing around for you. I know this thought all too well.

It comes up for me still to this day, but through the steps in this book, you will find your way through it. I've been here, too, so I know this must be costing you your connection with your lover, the deepest pleasures that wake you up in the morning, and even the confidence of your strength as a man.

Blessings, light, and love to you my friend. May all your dreams for a hard, sexy experience light your way to ultimate joy and peace.

Chapter 2

SHE STANDS IN YOUR SHOES

I stand with my bare feet in the sand. My body is fully aware of the sand giving away underneath me. I'm used to this feeling. When I think about it, my gut feels like it is made of quicksand falling away, and as I try with all my might to catch it or grab on to it with any certainty of success, it slips through my fingers like hopelessly trying to catch fog.

Warm teardrops roll down my cheeks with the hope that one will make it into her mouth to medicate the pain with the bitter taste of sorrow before being lost forever, falling to the shores of the ocean.

This is hard. No matter which way I turn. Nothing seems to be an easy step to take. Maybe, I think, I could just give up and that would take all the pain and suffering away forever. And just then, as I think I solved the problem with the easiest choice to just give up, a voice tells me, "If you choose to give up now, you will have to start from the beginning and go through all of this again. It won't be any easier and it might even be harder and more uncomfortable. Stay the course that has been set, and you will see that you are farther along than you could see from your current view. If you choose to gamble and start over, we honor that too, but know you will be faced with the same exact challenges just with different costumes and flavors of discomfort."

This is not what I wanted to hear. But I got the message loud and clear because I had already in my short life seen this to be true.

This is my story. The dark night of my soul hit me right when I thought my life was about to soar. I was twenty-six. I graduated from college with a degree in the theatre arts with an emphasis in acting, directing, and theatre public relations.

The year before I graduated, my university hired me to be an artist in residence for a program called Artpath. This was an organization that put artists into local schools to teach teachers how to incorporate the arts into the curriculum. The idea was to have the artist demonstrate teaching the art to the students so the teachers could learn from a professional in real classroom settings how to teach the art themselves, instead of trying to learn a new artform in a weekend workshop then go try to teach it well.

I loved that job, but it was not easy by any means. Have you ever had someone other than the head teacher come into a classroom and try to teach you? Substitute teachers are notoriously in the difficult position of coming into a hostile environment. Well, I fit into the same category as the substitute in the eyes of the students. If I didn't stay ahead of the power struggle the students would eat me alive.

I wasn't trained as a teacher. I was trained as an actor. As an actor I had to develop the skill of keen observation of the human condition and become courageously vulnerable at the drop of a hat. For some reason, throughout my life, I was given teaching positions that I took to like a fish to water.

You might be wondering how this all relates to me and your erectile dysfunction journey. Good question.

Thanks to this job, I found my way to you and the work I do today.

The work I did teaching kids the art of creative dramatics was the beginning of developing the healing techniques to heal sexual dysfunction. Instead of calling it creative dramatics, what I actually taught the kids and the teachers was the art of creative problem solving or creating something from nothing. Which is, in my twenty-two years of doing this work, a magical path to healing.

When parents would come up to me after a performance where their emotionally disturbed child was up on stage with all the other children from the school performing instead of hiding under the table, they just couldn't believe it.

"How did you do it?" they would ask. "No one has ever gotten him to do that. You are a miracle worker."

At this point, I realized I was onto something. I made the decision to study and create a healing modality that transformed lives which suffered from challenges that had no known medical solution.

I love people, and the littlest people on the planet are my biggest loves. To see a little kiddo suffering is hard for me to witness. I was motivated to find a method to heal the suffering of these precious beings so they would grow up happy, healthy and living the best lives possible. Being an adult was hard enough; I couldn't imagine what their lives would be like if they carried childhood trauma into adulthood.

One of the most profound things I learned in my work is that for the deepest level of healing, you need to be held as sacred and revered as a precious being. No matter what or who you are right now – a husband, a father, a CEO, a doctor, a surfer, a boyfriend, or a lover – you are and always will be sacred and divine. If you feel into the reverence of that statement you will feel in your heart and soul that you are precious. There is no one in the world like you and that alone is to be revered and honored in you.

I honor that first and foremost when working with my clients. This level of respect is where I start. I encourage you to start here with yourself and then give this gift to others. Most of us relate to each other without this level of reverence, instead believing the stories we tell ourselves about the person we think they are or think we are for ourselves. In this book I pray that you will find a deep reverence for yourself, as I have developed for myself, my clients and others in my life.

I didn't always have this reverence for myself or others. I was quite angry, bitter, and hostile to myself at times. Which I had no idea would be so damaging to my body and spirit. But the more I studied and practiced psychology, ontology, anthropology, hypnosis, tantra, and shamanism, the more I found all roads start here.

I went to work, throwing myself into creating what I called drama therapy using my first love, drama, with my second love, psychology, to see what I could do to heal people and make the world a better place. This is an important component to the work we will do together because I will train you to be a master of creation. In this book you will learn how to hypnotize your body to be what you want to be.

Don't worry about this all making sense right now. Just know that I will walk you through these steps and get you to where you want to go. Most people don't know what hypnosis really is. Most of us think hypnosis is a trick done on stage where someone else snaps their fingers and takes over the functions of the other persons body. But actually hypnosis is very simply anything that gets a person into a trance state or state of relaxation that gets the conscious mind set aside so the subconscious mind can be reprogrammed to function in a desired way. In chapter 9, I call the subconscious part of the brain your OS (Operating System).

Just like the computers OS, your subconscious is working in the background executing programs that were created by a much younger you who didn't have the knowledge or experience you have at your current age. The lessons in this book will start you on a path to take charge of your OS so you can get better at updating your programs yourself instead of having the default, out of date, programs run the show. The new term for this kind of work is Neurolinguistic Programming (NLP). Once you get the hang of this you will see that it will help you in ways beyond ED.

As I did my research and fine-tuned my results, I found that all the modalities of healing that had the biggest impact and longest holding results used the same principles, exercises and techniques that I studied to get into character as an actress and performer. You see, in order to be believable to an audience a performer does more than pretends to be someone else. A performer becomes that character and takes on the state of the person they are depicting so that they can react naturally to the moments on stage with the other performers they are telling the story with. Getting out of state and out of character is just as important as getting in. So performers need to develop a keen flexibility to create state change when needed. Below is a list of what I've learned to do this process and is analogous to the healing modalities to get you started on this journey to heal your body from ED.

- Be in the present moment.
- Authentically react to the person you are with.
- Be courageously vulnerable with your partner and audience and they will love whatever you do. Even if you mess up.

- Stand on a foundation of trust, respect, and safety and you can create anything your heart desires.
- Clean up any messes as soon as you notice you've created a mess, so the other person doesn't have to do the work for you or protect himself from you.
- Create from nothing.
- Fill your creation with Heart and Spirit.
- Let yourself soar.
- How you do anything is how you do everything.
- Don't play the end of the scene at the beginning. Be right where you are and your next action will be clear.
- The path of mastery is a mountain without a top. Stop searching for the top and put one foot in front of the other, baby steps will get you where you want to go. Enjoy the journey with honor and respect. For we know not what we are blind to.
- The universe works in mysterious ways.
- When in doubt improve and do the best you can.
- Forgive yourself for your own humanity and give others the same gift. We are all doing the best we can.

As my career took off, I was simultaneously insecure with my sexuality. This was problematic since I had to be comfortable portraying sexual characters. It got harder for me as I realized I had sexual dysfunction issues. That was more than twenty years ago. I had a story playing over and over in my mind that I was icky, not desirable, gross, and damaged goods.

I solved sexual dysfunction for myself. I consider my problem now, when I look back at it, to be erectile dysfunction, most people don't know about the female anatomy of arousal. Women have the same amount of erectile tissue as a man, it's just not so obvious because it is mostly inside. Until, that is, it gets erect and engorged, at which time the vulva puffs up and pushes open and out. As one can observe with other mammals (dogs, cats, primates, etc.) in heat. This was not something I was ever taught by conventional sex education.

The problem with sex education is that it is actually reproductive education, not sex ed, which is why there is a focus on producing an erection and orgasmic ejaculation. More on this later, but right now know that my stuff didn't seem to work either. I now regularly have multiple orgasms, sometimes without anyone even touching me, not even myself. And yes, even you men can use these methods in the book to have multiple orgasms.

My experience of erectile or sexual dysfunction back in my twenties was due to painful memories of #MeToo experiences at a young age. I thought there was something wrong with me. I felt like I was damaged goods, as if I were not worthy of being anyone's mate because, after all, I was not functioning.

From an early age, I was curious about the human body. I remember in class one time I was proud to know the anatomy of the human body better than anyone else. At the age of three, I was playing soccer, gymnastics, and superheroes with the boys at recess.

Back when I was a kid, I loved to watch shows like *The Six Million Dollar Man* and *The Bionic Woman*. I wanted to be strong and powerful enough to be able to lift a car up off someone if I had to. I loved what my body could do. It felt as if it could do anything I tried.

At the age of twelve, I would listen to the radio at night as I went to bed. One night, I picked up an L.A. station with a German lady called Dr. Ruth. She is a famous sex expert who talks openly about sexual pleasure being important in one's life. And that the word sex in Hebrew means to know each other.

I learned a lot from her at an early age. She has a way of talking openly about taboo topics your parents wouldn't even want to talk to you about. From what she taught her radio listeners, I learned how to masturbate and what to do when I touched a lingam. She openly gave instructions on how to stroke a man and how to stroke yourself for sexual satisfaction.

I like to think that I follow in her footsteps and take her mission to the next level where I help others know themselves so they can know one another by having the hard conversations and making it safe to discuss with me first, and then teaching you how to have these conversations with a partner.

But even with this amazing sex doctor setting such a strong example of comfort with the subject I still felt so icky about sex. I started to fake the orgasms, fighting with myself over this internal struggle. Later in life I even left perfectly good men because I couldn't admit to the shame and disgust, I felt about my own body.

The negative self judgement got so bad I fantasized about ending my suffering by walking out into the ocean to end it once and for all. I had panic attacks. I would leave my partner in the middle of lovemaking out of fear they would find out the truth about me.

I couldn't cum. I didn't know how to make my body work and I was convinced that there was something wrong with me. I thought I would never be loved by a man. I was confused and suffered for years when I finally met a lover who held me and guided me to orgasms that made me sing. Now look at me – I've become a modern-day sex coach supporting my clients have healthy sex lives like my mentor, Dr. Ruth.

This was just one of many hero's journeys I had the privilege of taking in this life. I'll sprinkle them throughout the book to guide you on yours. Along the way, we will find out how our male and female erections are affected in similar ways. We'll learn some yummy anatomy of arousal for men and women.

I love finding healthy solutions to problems. I'm committed to making a difference with you and your lovers. I know how difficult it is to discuss intimacy because I do it every day with clients and my own partners, friends and family members. It takes a commitment to love yourself, respect your wants desires, needs and boundaries, along with the practice of trust and courage to be vulnerable in the uncomfortable. I know because I had to do all of those things to write a book about a topic hard to talk about. I use my own tools when things get hard. I still have moments where I don't know if I can handle what is in front of me. But now after years of practicing using the tools I'm sharing with you it is easier and more natural to be free, be empowered, and vitally alive. All this is to say that being human doesn't ever go away, but if you follow these steps it gets easier every day to be free of suffering and have power in the face of anything that comes your way.

Chapter 3

BE A BEACON OF LIGHT IN SOMEONE'S DARKNESS

You and I are going to walk your journey together. I'm going to be like the sexy female version of Gandalf the Grey – Sequoia the Tree Goddess. When you need me most, I'll be right there. We're going to take one step at a time and build skills, knowledge, and mastery.

What got me through was having a simple process to follow while simultaneously being guided by mentors and coaches to show me things I was blind to that blocked my path. Now, I've assembled all that into this book to get you through it as I did and provide tools that can sustain your change. If I could, with my big dramatic plans to walk out into the ocean, get off that ledge to have a yummy thriving sex life today at the age of forty-eight, you can do this, too. I got you.

My method is simple and straightforward. To get the most out of the book, start from the beginning and move through each chapter. After you've completed steps in the chapters, you will start to see you have a toolbelt of ways to climax with lots of pleasure and ease. This will be your superpower in the bedroom.

Once you've gone through a step, you will add several steps together and use it as it serves you in any order (freestyle) in the bedroom. You might even teach your partner and really blow their mind. Practicing and staying the course to your beacon of light will be just as important as your belief in yourself, and before you know it magic will happen before your eyes. Like a tree reaching for the ray of sunlight, your body wants to grow and develop these skills. You just need to get out of its way.

In the beginning, my steps are going to seem too simple to be the difference that will make all this hard stuff turn into the hard stuff, if you know what I mean (wink wink, nudge nudge). But trust me, I've had the pleasure of guiding hundreds of people, including myself, through this, and once you get out of your own way, your body will start to respond automatically and go beyond anything you could have imagined when you got tossed into this hero's journey called erectile dysfunction.

Here's how it is going to go: First, we will assess your situation by looking at your Sexual Operating System (SOS). This is connected to your Relationship Operating System (ROS), but not the same. This is when you get to assess where you are, where you came from, and where you are going in the context of your SOS inside of your ROS. This is important because we are relationship beings.

Second, we will get you connected to your body and how it reacts to your SOS/ROS. We will do exercises to create connections to specific areas of the body that will be important to develop mastery in utility and functionality. Just like when you start using a new muscle, it doesn't work the way you dream it would work. It takes time and practice. You will develop that strength with the exercises in this book. This is where we learn and practice how your physical body functions in arousal. The byproduct of this work on yourself is that you will become a better lover to your partner because all the things I teach you about your body can be applied to your partner's body, too.

Third, we will uncover what is in the way of your erection being automatic and in the free flow of life's turn-on. This is heart-on work. We will clean out all the experiences of the past that have a kill response to your erection. Erectile dysfunction is directly connected to how well your heart is doing its job, not just blood circulation. The heart is the center of blood flow, energy flow, and emotional flow, and the intention of creation is the job of your sexual center. If you don't put your heart in what you are creating (e.g., baby, job, relationship, project, art, career, erection) then that thing will not come to full form. We will uncover and clear out all the old to create a new experience, bringing you back to the energy of a teenager.

Fourth, you will be free and open, which will allow you to learn lovemaking techniques to practice on yourself. I call this self-honoring (masturbation). You will also practice with a partner. You will learn a stroke that will help with circulation, to expand how much orgasm you can handle, and how to awaken the sleeping giant from his winter's slumber. Practicing these on a regular basis will be sexy, yummy, and quicken the body's erectile response the more you do it.

Finally, you will learn a variety of well-being practices that you can try. See if they give additional support to your experience of pleasure while you work the process above. The most important thing to remember is that it took years for your body to stop doing an automatic response to a stimulation. The reversal will take time for sure, but the results will surprise and delight you if you stay the course and trust your body's intelligence. Give the physical part time and space to solidify the healing we do together.

Please beware of pitfalls, don't plant the seed then pull the seed out of its soil to check on it and conclude it's not working. This is a time to trust yourself, trust the process, trust that these ancient techniques have stood the test of time, and with guidance, you can also master your Heart-On to Hard-On pathway to an amazing sex life and connection with your partner. The journey of sex is, as Dr. Ruth describes it best, for two people to know each other. Let this be what has you know yourself and your partner deeper.

I want to be clear with you; I'm not a medical doctor who will prescribe drugs or medical procedures. If there are aspects of what you are dealing with that require medical procedures and tests, you will figure that out along the way. I work with medical specialists who I can refer you to if you need to get opinions about your physical functionality. But in the beginning, you don't need to go to that drastic of a step.

If you are already under the care of a medical doctor for this issue, then please stay with them while we work together you continue to be monitored. Doctors often refer clients who need the work I do to me. I help them get to the next level without medical intervention.

The medical side of erectile dysfunction is real, and I honor that, but the emotional, psychological, spiritual, and subconscious side of the way our bodies work are not fully understood in Western medicine. This is where my understanding of Eastern and shamanic medicine comes into play. And why medical doctors send their clients to me or even come to me as clients themselves. You might be surprise at how many doctors and medical specialists I see in my practice. I know I was surprised at first.

The mystery of the mind, body, spirit connection has been passed down by shaman and healers of ancient traditions for thousands of years. What science is just now discovering and proving is that the ancient traditions knew way more than modern practitioners perceived initially.

My work brings these two together in the most sexy, fun, and yummy ways. I have spent my life dancing the fine line – the razor's edge I like to call it – between modern medicine and mystical healing techniques. Along the way, I have walked the path many times from healing myself from Lyme disease, to brain injuries, broken bones, and even my own sexual dysfunction.

I use these techniques to compete in triathlons, to come to peace with having had four precious babies die inside my body, as well as mourning the death of beloved family and friends. As I edit this book, I am healing a broken foot without pain. Believe it or not, the steps in this book have the potential to heal more than ED, as I am a testament to.

If you take on the steps in this book, even the hardest challenges in life will become your greatest teachers and will give you pleasure beyond your wildest dreams. You will be the master of your universe, the way you were designed to be for yourself and others around you.

You will have people magnetized to you. Your partner will want to know what you are doing so they can have what you have. You will be charming, loveable, desirable, authentic, sexy, and a mystery that others will want to discover, get close to, and know. You will be living the dream and want to share as I do every day how life can go from "life's hard" to "OMG please do that again."

Please know I love you, even if I've never met you before. As you read this book, a spiritual connection is made between us. I do this work because I love people beyond words or social norms. I'm a lover first and foremost. I love that you have come to face your fears, frustrations, and challenges.

I'm also tenacious. I won't listen to reasons and excuses that are disempowering contexts for why your situation is different and you just don't understand. You will get both with me and you will learn to like the lover and warrior in me. I'm going to be straight with you. I often cry with clients as I get moved by what we are accomplishing together.

But through it all, I intend for this book to support you. All I ask of you is that you don't give up and that you keep getting back up, and you will be amazed by what we have accomplished.

Chapter 4

HOW DID I END UP HERE?

"As soon as we control where awareness goes we control where energy flows. As soon as we control where energy is flowing we control what is manifesting in our life. And meditation is the art and science of directing awareness."

~ Dandapani ~

John and Martha met in medical school through a connection of both their parents. John adored Martha from day one and knew that she was going to make a wonderful wife, partner, and mother to his children.

Neither one of them had sex before they were married. Both of their families were traditional, so they had never had sex with anyone else before their wedding night. Their non-sexual connection allowed them to know that their relationship was solid from the beginning, outside of the bedroom.

This came in handy as their sex lives took an unexpected turn toward dysfunction. It turned out that Martha had unbearable pain with penetration. So bad that they couldn't have sex for years. Many of the couples I work with have never been taught sexuality and eroticism before marriage. Then, when they get married and sex is hard to do, they spend two to three years not being intimate with each other.

Sometimes it's the husband who has functionality issues, and sometimes it's the wife. Plus, there's pressure from the families to produce offspring, new careers to manage, and ladders to climb.

In this situation, Martha experienced extreme pain whenever they tried to have sex. John, a gentle, loving partner shut down his masculine desires to prevent hurting her; they stopped having sex, except to conceive, even though they both wanted it and kept searching for answers for how to make her body work sexually.

Twenty-five years into their struggle and no resolution to Martha's problem, John now had full-on erectile dysfunction. He was happy but lived a middle-of-the-road level of pleasure in life, no big extremes high or low. He threw himself into his work and became head of surgery at a hospital, well respected, and reliable.

They had enough sex to produce three children, but after that stopped, due to the pain. When the kids were grown, and they found they had time to focus on each other they decided to try tantra to solve this problem once and for all.

This is how they found me, a tantra educator and sexual healer.

Our first session we sat and they shared their story, vulnerably going over all they had been through together. I was in awe of how close they were. I could see how much John loved this woman. Step one is to become consciously aware of where you are on your journey in the present moment, I told them, to be witnessed and seen exactly where you are and where you aren't.

Once we set a marker in the present, we could look with curiosity and empathy instead of shame or blame. All the while, I was observing their patterns, beliefs, contexts from which they viewed their situation, all the little nuances that make up what I call a person's Relationship Operating System (ROS) and Sexual Operating System (SOS). As they shared, I repeated to them what I heard them say so I knew I was getting their communication and so they felt heard, understood, and valued. I then acknowledged who they were being for each other and gave reverence for their journey.

I could see their nervous systems relax and open to receive the gentleness of the session and to share the harder stuff to reveal. I explained that over our lives we accumulate past wounds that are never healed and are just pushed under or glossed over. We are truly the walking wounded. I often joke the reason zombie movies are so popular is because if we don't heal those wounds, we are actually the walking dead, dragging around bodies that don't work anymore. Our skin bags are driven without consciousness, able to feed but not able to regain life.

The wounds are where the life force energy is getting sucked out of the system and fed like alimony payments to upsets and trauma that are long past. Caroline Myss a well know medical intuitive says in her book *Why People Don't Heal and How They Can* that many of us are attached to the wounds of our lives for different reasons and use these excuses to not move forward, but rather stay in what's comfortable and safe.

The way I like to describe Myss's teaching is to imagine you are born as a whole complete circle. After a while the circle gets a chip taken out of it, then it gets a little hairline crack and then a big hole in the middle, and so on and so on. If these little bumps and nicks don't get healed when they are small, they get bigger and fester, and before you know it your wholeness looks like swiss cheese and is losing its integrity to stay whole. This is leaking life force energy out of the holes and cracks and spending energy you don't have to waste to barely function and survive.

If you want energy to go to an area for healing, the first step is to stop paying alimony to the past. This might require forgiveness, empathy, and understanding where there was regret, loss and anger. An easy way to start this process is to acknowledge that everyone in the situation was doing the best they could at the time. Have unconditional acceptance exactly the way it is and exactly the way it isn't. Now that there isn't energy feeding the wound, the healing can begin to grow life again. Mother Nature is very resourceful, if something is not growing it is decaying.

The Japanese mending practice of kintsugi is our next step in the healing process. This is where a broken ceramic is mended by being put back together with gold to represent that those things in life that bang us up are what make us precious and more valuable and beautiful.

Hemingway said, "The world breaks everyone and afterward many are strong in the broken places." If we take time to sit in reverence of these broken places, we can transform them into a life we love.

As I shared this practice with them, I had John and Martha lay together on the bed with him spooning her with his right hand on her heart and his left hand on her second energy center, where she had so much pain and experiences of being broken. In this position John's second chakra got to warm up to her buttocks and I had both of them practice squeezing and pumping their own pubococcygeus, or PC, muscles to activate their mutual arousal and desire. The PC muscles are often exercised by doing Kegels to strengthen them for men and women. But just as important as strengthening is relaxing them, especially for Martha's situation of too much tension in this area.

For woman that are learning to release I like them to imagine their vulva is like an octopus extending down and out to wrap itself around its desired lingam. This visual helps to allow the yoni to be free to let go and relax. Most of us have no idea how tense and uptight we are in our genitals.

In our second session we worked for hours on seduction, turn-on, male-female energy, and the cycles of arousal. I taught Martha how to stroke John, so his lingam got circulation to increase and start to respond. The sweet space we all held in the session was set with the work we did in the previous session where we took great care for each other and mended the wounds with the golden intimacy practice.

As Martha was massaging John's wand she was pumping and getting her juices in her sex to grow and feeling the pleasure her hands were experiencing by worshiping her beloved husband. I instructed her to gaze into his eyes and acknowledge who he is for her and their family. These simple statements were getting embedded deep in his subconscious and his nervous system where his autonomic nervous system would mend like Kintsugi all the places he might not even know he had wounds.

We were together for four hours laughing, sharing love stories and going slowly and lovingly into the three stages of touch, arousal, and S.E.X. M.A.G.I.C exploration. John's lingam was reacting beautifully to her sexy new way of being and so was her sex. His shaft was having a hard time holding the blood flow so I taught her how to hold her pincher fingers at the base of his wand front and back. This will hold the blood in the lingam instead of going out, but the blood flow can still get in the wand resulting in a stronger and stronger erection manually that tips over to his body's natural response of fullness.

Her other hand, covered in lots of warm coconut oil, pulled the blood up the shaft to the head moving the circulation up to the tip. When he was feeling fully turned-on and she was feeling full and juicy we practiced different positions that would make their arousal grow and they experience a beautiful full release and gentle bliss.

After the session with me, they were able to both open and experience pleasure with each other. After three sessions, he was able to penetrate her and climax. He got sensation back in his lingam and had a full release.

His heart practically leapt out of his chest; he was so happy. He didn't think he'd ever have that experience. His love for his beautiful wife that he had been through thirty-five years with was enormous and filled with so much gratitude.

They still practice regularly the lessons in this book. They claim it's some of the most fun and sexy homework they've ever had. And they are so glad to spend time with each other exploring their bodies and all the things the body can do.

It's so exciting to see couples light up and fall in love with this work. Truthfully, it's sacred sexuality and sensuality training for adults that didn't get that from their families and community. So many people remark after learning these lessons that we really need this at an early age. Ancient traditions taught that we are sensual, sexual beings. We are driven to create. That's why we have careers and jobs and always things to do. We were made in the image of the Creator and therefore we are Creators. With a capital C. Our task here on earth school is to practice and get good at creating and manifesting into the physical form from which we get pleasure out of imagining.

It is important for the connection to spirit be well established, as well as the connection to the earth through a trusted ground. The energy flow must be secure in order for the imagined result to show up in the full physical expression. This is a sacred practice that is to be respected.

But when we were kids and we experimented, we didn't know anything and we fumbled in the dark, not sure how it all works. And because there was no one to guide us, we started to think that there was something wrong with us. Just as I thought about myself. I didn't realize that it was normal to not get sex right at the beginning. Don't give up or think that there is something wrong with you. We really do need the Dr. Ruths, sex and relationship healers like myself, and other tantra teachers like Charles Muir and Margot Anand to show you what your body can do.

When people lived in tribes, we would learn these lessons from the wisdom of the elders. It was passed down as sacred and practiced with a beautiful reverence. This is what I experience when I teach people about pleasure and how it makes you healthy, happy, and high on life. We don't need to get that out of a little blue pill. Our bodies are totally equipped with the chemicals in our brains ready to fire.

The autonomic nervous system loves to be turned on. We have to stop shaming the human race for being sexual. If we weren't sexual, we'd never get anything done. The second chakra is the creation energy of the whole system. It creates a new human from nothing. That is power. But it needs a place to land and find a home. Both energy and physical form are just as important as the other. I see energy form and physical form as analogous to feminine and masculine.

That's right, the masculine and the feminine are equally important to the other. This is the law of polarities reconciled. We need each other to be courageously vulnerable, to trust, respect, and keep each other safe. If we teach sex ed from this perspective, it becomes S.E.X. instituting (Sacred Experience of Xstasy).

When we teach it this way, the youngsters experimenting will more likely show the respect this magical process, to know another, is intended to be. When this kind of reverence is shown, there comes responsibility, integrity, authenticity, and leadership. Then they would choose to participate to have more good feeling experiences and stay away from people who wouldn't take the respect and care for the act as sacred to them.

We touch the divine when we connect to another person naked to the universe. They see all of us. In-to-me-see (intimacy) is standing naked in front of another with all your gifts and flaws, saying, "Here I am, exactly as I am, and exactly as I'm not. This is what I have to offer. I love myself enough to know if you don't want me for who I am right now, then I'm fine loving myself in wholeness until I come to a person who does."

I love myself that much. My journey is a long one, but I wouldn't have it any other way because I'm learning so much about why we are here and how to find pleasure in the moment.

The hero's journey you never wanted. Here is a way through the process. Freedom from the constraints of the life lived until this point that has created a default life I didn't ever want. Freedom is the result of getting present and acknowledging where I am on the journey. The journey needs to be acknowledged to have respect and reverence for the step on the path that you find yourself on.

How did I end up with ED? This is not supposed to happen this way to me.

So how did you get here? And what do you do now that you are dealing with ED? The how and the why are less important to the success of the journey than your commitment to doing whatever it takes to get you to the result you are here for. Climax without hard work. I know it's hard right now and you are truly on the search for a way through it to success.

I asked these same questions about a health issue I had to deal with a few years back. I had a head injury, the third one in my life. This was hard for me because I'm in love with learning, teaching, and creating. When my brain wasn't working the way I was used to, I was devastated and deeply depressed.

I felt alone. I was confused at why this was happening to me. Did I do something wrong to have this happen to me? For the first time in my life I decided to not run away from the discomfort of the situation. Instead, I chose to sit deep in the experience and not try to fix it. In order to get present, and after consulting my neurologist and team of doctors and healers, I took a year off work to heal my brain.

When I asked my doctors what kinds of healing modalities or remedies they use to heal the brain they said, "We could give you these pills that might help." Or "The only thing we can prescribe is to stop any stress on the brain and give it time to heal." None of them knew how long I would need and what my path would entail.

The time off was from screens and complicated tasks. Well anyone who knows me would tell you that not working or having a full schedule is not me. I do not like to sit still and I love my big projects with lots to do. The idea of taking long periods of time off and not do anything was just as hard for me as the actual mental dysfunction I was experiencing from the head injury.

I had a hard adjustment period. I resisted it. I fought it. I denied it. Until it became clear I have no choice but to prepare. I went to work for a few months getting all my work accounts handled. And off I went. At first it was only a month, but as I was now able to really see clearly what I was dealing with a month turned into a year.

This was the year that changed my life. This book is the result of my discoveries to heal my brain. Along the way I found how to heal men and women from their bodies failing them too.

Now you might be saying, "But you are talking about the brain and I'm dealing with my lingam working." You will see along the way how they are connected. I'll say quickly that the brain is a major contributor to your orgasmic experience. What most people don't know is that our brains can be rewired, and new neurological pathways can be laid down with the ancient healing practices of tantra yoga. The exciting thing for me is that I have been able to transmute something so hard for me that I wasn't sure I would get through it, into my ability to help others the way I was able help myself.

> *"Change only comes when you put tools into daily practice."*
>
> ~ *Unknown* ~

> *"The beginning of mastery is; that what you are mastering at least comes up for you immediately when you have failed with what you are mastering, that is to say, you consistently immediately catch yourself."*
>
> ~ *Landmark Worldwide* ~

Extra Credit: Please read *Mastery* by Robert Greene to understand why the commitment to mastery is so important to healing erectile dysfunction. The principles from this book are major tenets of my book. To fully understand the practice of mastery, I know no other source than my all-time favorite book, *Mastery* by Robert Greene. In this book you will learn the elements to master anything. This book is recommended reading for all my students and clients who work with me. It provides a concrete and researched analysis of mastery from case studies of historical and modern masters in a variety of fields, cultures, and stages of mastery as a path with no end. In other words, mastery is a mountain without a top. When you choose to take on mastering anything it is my opinion that all of us have everything we need right in our own lives if we can start from right where we are.

The best way I've found to read this and lots of books during this process is to listen to audiobooks. I don't know about you, but my life is so full that I don't have many windows of time to just sit and read a whole book without lots of distractions. I get my reading in while I'm driving, flying, waiting in the airport, walking at lunchtime, or sunbathing on the beach when it is too sunny to see the page, but I can focus on listening to the book being read to me.

Get Grounded

My tantra master Charles Muir, with whom I trained intensely, taught me from day one the first thing you need to do in any situation is ground and connect to where you are right now in time and space. This is the function of the first energy center, also known as the first or base chakra. The energy and need connecting with this energy center provides the sensation of certainty, security, and contact with the physical form. This is also the foundation that your entire system (body, mind, and spirit) needs in order to function or create workability.

This is the experience of being grounded in the physical world and in your body. This is the start of healing. Just as oxygen is one of the most important first steps in health of the primordial systems of the body, grounding and becoming certain of where you are is the first step in your hero's journey. Think of the movies that use the principle of the hero's journey as a story line.

Star Wars is one most of us know. The first scenes where we find our hero's journey has begun are ones where he or she are on their knees, not sure how to get out of the hard situation they found themselves in. Often they were going about their life, doing what they always did – comfortable and fine.

Then, when the hero's journey shows itself, a guide comes along with the option to assist them through it. Unfortunately, most heroes of these stories reject the journey and the guide at first reaction. Only to come back around when there doesn't seem to be any other options than to succumb to the journey they never asked for.

Congratulations. Here we are. I am someone who has gone through the hero's journey multiple times. Each time I find more of myself and ways in which all of us could apply this concept to our lives.

A quote from Eckhart Tolle's book *A New Earth* has help me in indescribable ways. That quote is simple to say but not easy to practice, but if you just use it, the miracle of this statement will be profound. It says this, "This too shall pass."

If you think about this practice, which I highly recommend to try for yourself, you will see that it is the perfect reminder, whether things are going really badly or really great. Wrap your consciousness around that for just a moment. Notice and even write down in your journal what thoughts, feelings, and emotions come up for you around this idea.

Even when the tough gets tougher, you will see that "this too shall pass." Stay the course. The only way that the journey gets dangerous or fails to work is if you attempted to jump ship or abandon your path. There really is nowhere to go, so it actually creates more work by getting distracted or wooed by the idea of, "if only I could get to where I want to go without going through this part." If you stay the course, you will see that which doesn't kill you makes you stronger.

You are in the perfect place. I witness your struggle and the difficulty of getting through or at least to the other side of what you are dealing with. The technology in this book is innovative and yet simple and powerful.

The more you give yourself up to the process in your own personal way the more you get out of the journey. Be good to yourself along the way. Set up a reward system that helps you stay the course and celebrate the gifts of this sacred experience of life lived full out. I love you, even if I don't know you personally. You got this. I'm right by your side and will root you on to the homecoming of your future where you climax without hard work.

If we look at my story as a road map to get you to "climax without hard work" it might seem counterintuitive to you right now, but you can't get to where you want to go with more hard work. The first step of grounding is to stop.

Stop

Where awareness goes, energy follows. And energy in your lingam is what is going to get you hard. You control where your awareness flows and you control your energy flow.

You control what you manifest/create in your life. What you manifest is an engorged, fully hard erection that is automatic and gets the job done.

The first thing to do is stop. In stillness of the physical and mental body, you can feel the subtleness of the energy body. Stop the chatter in your head. Stop trying to fix it. Stop trying to ignore it. Stop spinning. Stop trying anything. Just stop and allow.

I like to use the word pause. Pause is a temporary stop that will give you a chance to get your bearings. What are we trying to do by getting our bearings? We are wanting to observe. To look at everything with eyes wide open.

You actually need to know where you are before you can start a journey. If you were going to take a trip from California to New York, and you were actually in Memphis, Tennessee, you would get lost because your starting location doesn't match the map that works for California to New York. Stop and assess where you are.

Exercise 4.0

Please pull out your journal or recording device to make an entry.

Answer this question in your journal for yourself: Where am I on this ED journey?

Set a timer for five minutes and write everything that comes to mind without editing or correcting. (I'd like you to write with the intention of just dumping all your thoughts on the page. No assessing what you write or the thoughts that come out. Just put your pen to paper and empty your mind on the page. If you find you're stopped and don't know what to write, then you write exactly that. "I don't know what to write. It is hard to find things to say.")

Breath

When we focus on breath, it is hard to doing anything else. This is why most meditation practices use breath to find presence. Eckhart Tolle teaches us in his work that if a person was to simply put awareness to his breath every day for one full year, he will find enlightenment. And here is the good news: Tantra has been cited in many ancient philosophies to be one of the quickest ways to enlightenment. Let's see if we can discover why together.

Why breath? And what kind of breathing do you mean?

I could just say don't ask, just do. But that wouldn't give you a place to focus or a purpose to use the breath for. I'm going to shed some light on what the breath is doing for our work together.

In tantra and other modalities of meditation, breath is used to bring awareness or focus or presence to the task at hand. As I stated, the task at hand is to empower your wand of light to be alive and energized so that you can have freedom to climax with ease.

Exercise 4.1: Grounding Tree Meditation

Close your eyes.

Notice the kind of breathing you are in right now.

In your mind's eye, imagine that you have roots at the base of your spine where your tail bone is.

Visualize those roots growing down through the floor of the room you are in, down into the earth's crust.

As you grow your roots deeper, thicker, and wider, imagine the foundation of your journey is being supported by the root system you are creating right now. You are growing your roots into the heart of the earth's energy core.

Now that you have reached the core, grow your roots around and around and around the core of the earth, really anchoring yourself in feeling grounded and centered and connected. (Anytime in life when you aren't sure what to do or what will help you in a challenging situation, simply replay this grounding meditation in your mind's eye and you will instantaneously ground yourself.)

Wherever you are in the breathing cycle exhale completely and leave yourself empty for two seconds.

Inhale the golden powerful energy from earth's core up the roots, up the spine to the top of your head and hold the breath.

Swallow to lock the breath.

Roll your shoulders back and down.

Be still in your physical body. (You will notice that when your body is still you can finally feel the energy that your awareness was looking for.)

Hold the breath as long as you can. Really stretch your lung capacity beyond your comfort zone. This will be a theme in this book I come back to again and again. Do your best and set aside any judgement and just be with the experience. Whatever the experience, it is perfect just the way it is and just the way it isn't.

When you are ready to exhale, set an intention to let go of all the things in your life that no longer serve you.

Now with an "ah" sound let go of the breath with the "ah" communicating the release and completion of the past. The carbon dioxide being released from your body is the byproduct of the past inhale that now needs to be exhaled from your body.

The exhale can also be identified as old dead air that is let go to make room for the new activities, new life, entering the body thanks to oxygen, the all-important life-giving element. When I studied alternative wellness modalities like homeopathy, nutrition, and exercise I learned one of the most important elements for health is oxygen.

If you think about it, we can live without food for several days, maybe a week. You can go without water for a few days. But you can only go without oxygen for a few minutes before you die. One of the ways you know how important something is to life is take it away. Therefore, oxygen is a major component in overall health and well-being, and if you increase oxygen intake and circulation you can heal the primordial imbalance bringing your body into balance and your body's automatic healing process can do its job. In other words, oxygen being present can heal. Breathing deeply and keeping the breathing going fills your whole body with new life.

Do a six-count inhale. Hold it for as long as you can. Then six-count exhale. Continue this process for two more times (or more if you are finding it feels beneficial).

Sound

The sound from your mouth is magical. It can be the magic sauce that you use to release deeply. All sound can help turn us on.

Have you ever held a cat when it is purring? The sound and vibration of the purr is intoxicating. When we meditate, the sound we make on the exhale vibrates through our whole body to dislodge the energy and past that is stuck in our body, mind, and spirit. It is our own personal sound healing tool. The sounds that we can make in our body help the release of ecstasy as well. More on that later. For now, practice with different sounds as you exhale and see what ones feel best.

Once you are grounded, you can move to cyclical breathing. Inhale for six seconds and exhale for six seconds. No beginning, no ending, just flow and bring awareness to your breath. Let all the thoughts that want to distract you float on by you like leaves on a river. No need to pick them up, just notice and leave them to go on their own way down the river.

Your job right now is to practice and develop willpower over your thoughts/ticker tape story running wild in your brain. To master letting thoughts float on by while meditating is to train your mind, body, and spirit to follow your intention or creation. You will find out why this is important as we put all the pieces together.

Journal Entry

Make a note in your journal of what you got from this exercise. What did you learn? What new experience happened because of the grounding meditation?

Willpower

To develop willpower or creation power, you must practice and apply what you learned from each practice. This is just like strengthening a muscle. Take it slow and do the exercises to strength this element. Here are three things to help develop willpower or creation power.

Practice these three methods with everyday happenings. Example: To finish the process of sleep, I make the bed. The process of breakfast is making it, eating it, cleaning it up. When we can have an empowered experience without forcing something to happen, we have freedom to create what we really want in life. Not just living with the default life where you don't know how you got there.

- Finish what you start.
- Finish well beyond your expectations.
- Finish and do a little more than you thought you were able to do. Pushing beyond your comfort zone makes you grow stronger.

Presence

How do we do what seems hard even when it looks like a better idea to give up and go back to wherever we were before we started this whole thing? Giving up really does look easier, but let's just take a good look at this. Can you go back?

Even if you had a magic wand, would you really want that old you back and all that comes along with that time in your life? If so, why?

Journal Entry

Really look at the answers that come to mind and make a note somewhere in a journal, the notes app on your phone, or grab a scratch paper from anywhere and write down all your answers that you hear.

Let me give you examples from hard times in my life that had moments where I wanted to give up, turn back, or curse that I didn't ask for them.

In my twenties, I was contemplating giving up on life. At twenty-six, I blew out my left knee while at my job as a theatre manager and PR for City Lights Theatre Company in San Jose, California. I finished my degree as a performer, director, teacher, and theatre PR. I worked four jobs and was on my own for the first time out of school.

The injury was stupid and didn't seem to be complicated. It wasn't that big of a deal on the outside looking in. But if I could compare it to what an experience of ED could be like, it was like you had just won the partnership lottery with the most gorgeous partner and had graduated to being married and all that you had focused our sights on was to get to the wedding bed. And once we were there in the heat and excitement of the event your lingam broke or stopped functioning the way you needed it to attain the goal of having mind-blowing wedding night sex.

Your whole life led to this and this is what you were left with. How could my body fail me at this most important moment? Well, that is exactly what I asked myself. See, my knee didn't just stop working; it messed everything up. I was an actress, dancer, director, teacher, creator. My tool was my body and now my body was not able to do all of the things I spent my whole life training to be able to do.

And what was worse is that all this came with the worst pain throughout my body that was exhausting to deal with. I couldn't sleep, lay down, or stand up. My hair hurt. My body couldn't enjoy being touched because it would throw me into pain. No one could figure out what was wrong with me. It seemed as if my body had betrayed me. I did everything I could to avoid the sensation of pain and betrayal.

I didn't have many options for how to fix the problem. I tried to get the surgeon to go back in and remove hardware that might be causing the problem, but that didn't work. I worked with a pain management doctor whose solution was to put me on anti-depression medications that made everything worse and took away one of my life's pleasures of eating spicy foods. Medications often have side effects that don't make sense. The meds also sedated me. I felt like a zombie and a ghost of myself. That seemed so much worse than the pain. After almost a year, I finally said no more anti-depressants. I tried self-medication with alcohol and cigarettes to numb the pain and to kill the spinning. I spun like this for years trying anything, but not getting anywhere. The stories spinning in my head were just as unbearable as the physical sensation. "I must be a bad person. I'm damaged goods. If only I had a body that worked. I'm all alone in this and no one will ever want me in this shape. I should just give up because there is no way out of this alive." Have you had thoughts like that about your lingam?

It was so unbearable that I just wanted to turn my body in for a new one that worked. I talked so badly to my body. I yelled at it. I even had thoughts of cutting off the leg that started the whole problem. I was on my knees, begging for a solution that would work.

I realized as I was at my lowest that, in fact, I didn't want to harm myself, but the whole time I wanted to live more than anything, and that I had to make some big changes in order to find my way to the other side of this situation.

I reached out for help from an ex-boyfriend who I knew would help me find a way through the darkest nights. He always listened when I need to be heard, understood and valued all I needed to do was ask for his help and be vulnerable. Jeff was there for me the night I admitted I had a problem that I couldn't fix on my own. I told him everything I hid from everyone. He was so loving and compassionate. Even though we were not together anymore, we loved each other, and he helped me stop the spinning by just acknowledging that I couldn't do this alone.

Once I stopped spinning, I found my way to solutions in magical ways. My boss at the time recommended that I go to a personal training and development program called the Landmark Forum. I wanted to have my life back so bad I was willing to try anything to heal my pain.

The program was not for people with pain or the problems I had. It was for big people with big lives. The way my life was going was more like big problems, but I wanted so badly to go back to healing with drama, therapy, and developing my work to make the biggest difference in the lives of others. But how was I supposed to do this if I was in a pain cycle all the time? I took a chance and went to the seminar.

Three twelve-hour days in a chair did not sound like a fun plan for a person who couldn't sit for five minutes without pain. But I did it anyway. If it didn't help with the pain, at least I would learn how to handle life and free myself to go back to school and get my master's or do something meaningful with my life.

The people who had to sit next to me were obviously annoyed by my inability to sit still and not fidget. My legs shook back and forth because it was the only way to distract from the pain. The first thing I learned in the course was that I had filters I viewed and thought of my life through. These filters were hard to hear with all the chatter in my head. The chatter I named the ticker tape of the stories about myself, about my situation, about people, wrongs done to me, wrongs I couldn't forgive myself for because I must be a bad person, regrets of anything and everything I had done or experienced that went wrong. And the list went on and on and on.

At some point, I was able to see the disempowering filters that were creating internal stories, which were making me suffer more than the actual pain itself. It was a miracle. The moment I was able to see the filter and the story that filter created, my legs stopped fidgeting and the pain disappeared. It was like magic.

How could this be? I was hooked and wanted more. I felt a rush of energy and had a love for life again, yet all I did was stop and get present to the difference between what was actually happening versus the story I told myself about what happened.

To really drive this home, the workshop leader took us through an exercise I had used to teach presence and vulnerability to my drama students. It was a trust game where you stand or sit with another person and just stare. No talking – just stare or eye gaze (a tantra witnessing exercise you will use). This might sound simple, but if you've ever tried it, it's not as simple as you would think.

The reason we do trust exercises in theatre classes or while rehearsing a play is to train the performers and production team to trust each other in the vulnerable tasks that are required for putting on a live performance. "The show must go on" is the motto of those who produce plays. Don't let anything take you away from getting the job done.

There is a powerful experience that happens when you stare into the window to another person's soul, the eyes. You can't hide anything, and neither can they. It is an exercise in being witnessed, courageously vulnerable, and naked. This alone will change your life because you will become a person over time that cleared all the crap out of your space so you could be witnessed.

By the end of the three-day course, I had my life back because I healed the internal pain that all the past wounds of my life caused that I was blind to. We as humans carry around shame, embarrassment, and destructive internal stories that kill our dreams and confidence.

I walked out of there having power over the shame, fear, and embarrassing stories I had about myself because they no longer had the disempowering meaning that debilitated me before. Let me be clear about what I'm sharing; the stories were still there floating in my mind like the leaves on the river image I shared during the meditation. I could pick up the thought and obsess about them but why? It no longer served me to have those thoughts waste anymore of my energy than they already had. No more paying alimony for the past that has been so unnecessarily painful and destructive to all my life plans. I cleared my past wounds. What I was left with was a blank canvas to create something totally new from nothing, as I taught my drama students to do.

But the piece I missed in the process that changed everything was the clearing of the past. Trying to create something new and exciting on top of old patterns and crap from the past is like putting icing on a poop pie and expecting it to taste like banana cream. No matter how much icing you put on it, you are still eating a pile of poop.

Years went by and I got through the chronic pain and had a new life, a marriage, and a new baby. But after the baby, all the pain was back. It appeared that something deeper was going on, especially when I lost my second baby at thirteen weeks of gestation. I really couldn't mess around because I had a baby and a husband to take care of. I needed to find a cure to the health problems.

I tried everything and finally came to chanting Buddhism to explore a deeper spiritual solution to getting through life. I took it on like an athletic training event. And that required sitting in chanting meditation one hour in the morning at 6:00 a.m., one hour at night, and if I had time, 1 hour in the middle of the day.

What I love about chanting Buddhism is that it feels as if you are doing something because you are chanting, but really it is just as if you are focusing on the breath. You train your mind to follow the awareness so you can manage your energy. Where you have awareness, energy flows. And we will be using this energy flow to turn you on and make you erect. Use powers of concentration to hold awareness.

The act of chanting is setting in motion the prayer and intention you create in your life and the world. Through the meditations I found clarity that lead to new actions I would have never seen to take which lead to a doctor that found my problem. I had Lyme disease. Boy, I did not see that coming. When I got that diagnoses it felt like someone had just told me I had cancer but not the kind that kills you, the kind that keeps you spinning in a pool of unresolvable pain where you wished to die. I used the chanting and daily prayer dedication to creating that I am cured of Lyme disease. What showed up was a result I didn't expect.

The healers and teachers to get me to a cured state of health and vitality arrived and we made it through together. I didn't heal overnight. It took work, time, and staying the course, but now, more than fifteen years later, I'm still free and clear of Lyme disease and the debilitating effects on my life and relationships.

If you created it, the universe wants you to have it. Just show up, do the meditations, and you will see the actions that are right for you to get through the valley of terror and the dark night of the soul like I did.

Exercise 4.2: Eye Gazing

One fun and connecting way you can practice presence is to eye gaze with your partner. Get lost in their eyes and see what you learn from them without saying anything. Just sit in front of you partner, hold hands, and connect eye gazes. You may do this while doing the grounding meditation above. You will be amazed at how connected you feel by just holding space for your partner to be witnessed by you. If you don't have a partner, I'd like you to pick something in nature to gaze into. Bring arousal and sensual awareness, and lessons of your Sensual Operating Systems patterns learned to your journal. This will help you to put new eyes on life and awaken to new actions.

New actions create new connections in the brain that create new life and new ideas all of which are required for new experiences and feeling vital and alive with growth and expansion. Sound yummy and arousing yet? I hope you are starting to see the connection to your erection but if not just try on what I'm teaching you and see for yourself. New neurological connections between the spirit, mind and body are required to transform anything going on with the body that you want to alter.

Now that you are grounded, aware, and present, where are you going to find answers to problems you are blind to? This is the challenge with the hero's journey. If you knew how to get through it yourself, you wouldn't need this book. The process we are experimenting with together and the journal entries will reveal the answers you never would have found on your original path.

Going back to my knee injury and chanting, when people ask me how I healed from Lyme disease, I start by answering, "With chanting Buddhism." They often look at me funny, but it's true. The chanting Buddhism got me to be still and listen to my innate intuition, which eventually led me to the cocktail of doctors who, in the end, were my team that helped me heal one baby step at a time. It didn't look at all like I thought it would. It didn't matter to me how I got there; I was just so grateful to have been cured of a disease that everyone was telling me was uncurable.

Now that you are well on your journey, how do you recognize when you're in a fight for your life or just a distraction trying to keep you from getting to the other side? Traps. One side is the winning and the other side is planning to do whatever it takes to prevent you from winning. This is how they win your energy. Imagine Frodo in *The Hobbit* and how badly the dark side wanted him to give up the path forward. The fog is the hardest because it feels like you can catch it, but in order to see through the fog you have to be the fog. Sit in it to catch it and all the lessons you can receive from the fog.

Now think about what you need to have a successful journey. Respect and pack for the trip. Prepare yourself and life for the journey. Start from right where you are, not where you wish you were. What items do you need to bring with you along the way that will keep you alive and on track? What abilities do you need in order to accomplish your goal for the journey?

- Be curious
- Be brave
- Be playful
- Be courageous
- Be willing to try anything
- Be love
- Be reverent
- Be a leader
- Be generous
- Be part of a community

Whether you join the "HARD Conversations with Sequoia" community or have a men's group, it must create a community around you of support. You don't get out of this alive without support. Please notice what kind of support I'm suggesting or insisting you find. Please look for and surround yourself with the people who will support your commitment to working through your hero's journey. Don't settle on what you think you can find. Find what you actually want from a clear present state of being.

This is not a time to allow anyone who would pull you away from your commitment. Think of these people as working for you or not working for you. No need to criticize them for who they are and what they do, just assess the relationship for supporting you with workability or not supporting you, as in not workable. Our community is created to support the kind of work we are all doing together. If you read this book while working through your ED solo and you choose to not use my support community, please find a men's support group that meets your needs that are unique to you.

Along the way, you are going to have more sex that is S.E.X., more pleasure while having this sex, and feel more than you ever have while working this process. Like Mr. Miyagi from *Karate Kid*, I might ask you to take an action that doesn't make sense to you where you are right now. But I promise, like the *Karate Kid*, it will all make sense when it all gets put together and applied.

If you are someone who knows that this is an edge of discomfort, then this is the perfect place for you to lean into the discomfort. Freedom is on the other side of this. Stay the course and know this:

I don't expect or want you to just believe me. I want you to try something that might be new for you. This has helped me in my journeys. Come to this with a beginner's mind, like a curious kid who takes it all in and tries it out. Imagine I'm asking you to try on a pair of shoes to walk this path for the next few months. If after you finish this book you feel my suggestions don't work for you, feel free to discard whatever doesn't work and keep what does. If this is the context for you during the journey, I promise you something new that you never expected will come to you that will get you to where you want to go. And along the way I hope you will find other books or talks or classes, mine or other teachers, that will confirm what you are learning. When we try on ideas without analysis, criticism, or trying to figure it out, we are surrendering. Be curious, creative, caring, compassionate, conscious, connected, and courageous.

What you might find from this is a path cleared, like fog evaporating, and if you pay attention to these signs, you will find your way. Just keep coming back to the process. When in doubt, call an accountability partner, from our community or the support community you have. I highly recommend a coach to work the process with you. This is the majority of the work just coming back to the process this is way easier than giving up and thinking you have to start all over. This is all part of the process. Remember, I've got you. More importantly, you've got this.

Chapter 5

HOW AM I GOING TO GET THROUGH THIS FAST AND EASY?

"If you want to find the secrets to the universe think in terms of Energy, Frequency, and vibration. Everything is made up of energy and is vibrating as a certain frequency."

~ Nikola Tesla ~

Energy is a precious resource for your journey. It is the special sauce that makes everything alive and vital. But what is energy? Where do you find it and how do you use it? I want you to imagine that you have bank accounts of energy in your body and the field around you. There are seven energy banks and it will be your responsibility to manage the input/investment and output. Be careful not to give it all away. This currency will be important as we get deeper into the process and also make sex much juicier and full.

The first law of thermodynamics is that energy can neither be created nor destroyed. It can only change forms. We are made up of energy that expresses itself in different forms throughout these seven banks. The banks correlate to the nerves going to the parts of the body these energy centers support. We already started working the energy banks with the grounding meditation in Chapter 4. By now, you will have found ways to practice the presence and awareness. The reason we do that piece first is because energy takes some practice to feel and learn to move. Energy, also known as chi or prana, is the life force that keeps us alive and full of life and vitality. When you master managing your energy, you become the creator of your universe instead of being a victim of a situation you had no say in.

I'm teaching you in this book to step into your power as a creator. Creations always start with energy. When we are born, we come in with all the energy we need to fuel the life purpose we are here for. If we are careless with spending our energy, the system breaks down and steals energy from other banks. It is important to understand the law of thermodynamics in relationship to what I'm teaching you. If it's true that you came into this life with a set amount of energy, then it is even more important to use it wisely.

But why are we talking about energy in regard to ED? Because you will master moving energy in your body so that you can bring back to life your body parts that have lost their energy flow. Please keep a beginner's mind around this and try what I'm sharing with you. A beginner's mind is a practice of choosing to see with new eyes a world you would otherwise see as just the same old thing you saw before. When you open yourself to see through the lens of new wonder and curiosity you can tap into new discoveries that someone who thinks they have seen and know everything is blind to. Energy moves quicker that the physical body. Some of the work we do together is being still in the body so we can feel the energy.

Here's a little understanding of energy and sexual activity. When a man has an orgasm with an ejaculation, the man's body collects all of the energy and sends it into the woman's body – a payment from all seven energy banks to power the life being created (baby) in the woman. It is equivalent to a man running a marathon. This is why when men ejaculate, they seem to roll over and fall asleep – because they just ran a marathon and their body needs to recover as they would if they ran a real race.

But what if you weren't on the path to create another human being, yet you still would like to have sex? The cool thing about this is that there are ways to move the energy raised in the act of sex so that it feeds your body instead of leaving and depleting. Let's do an exercise to practice this new idea.

Exercise 5.0: Moving Energy Exercise

Start with turning on one of my recorded meditation soundtracks for this one. (www.ItsHardBook.com/meditation) Begin with the grounding meditation from Chapter 4.

The energy you tap into at the core of the earth is the earth's donation to your life purpose.

Imagine a golden light is at the core of the earth and you move that energy by drawing it up from the roots to the top of your head. (Guess what's between the roots and your head – your lingam, which, as you remember, means "wand of light" in Sanskrit.) While you are pulling the energy from the earth up your body, visualize your wand filling with light. Pump your PC muscles (pubococcygeal or pelvic floor muscles) to help the awareness of the energy to go where you want it to go. When I imagine with my mind's eye that the energy is filling my sex (also known as yoni, Sanskrit for "sacred space") with light to bring awareness and life force energy, I see the golden light filling every last inch of my body and yoni with this energy like a glass of orange juice magically filling from the bottom of the glass and spilling over the top. The visualization helps bring the energy into the physical form from the ether.

Allow yourself to get tantalized by the flow or sparkling energy. Without touching yourself, fill up your lingam with golden healing light that will bring your lingam alive whenever you choose to create it.

Stay grounded, present, and aware of the flow and just notice sensations.

Remember that energy is the special sauce. It is not something that is taught in conventional sex ed or by parents who teach us the birds and the bees. But this is what transmutes what I call skin bag sex to soulful/empowered S.E.X. (Sacred Experience of Xstasy). This is the element that has more sensation than the friction of the body parts rubbing together. It is the extra juice that takes your experience from good to mind-blowing. At first, your body will adjust to the new experience and the sensation of energy. Like bringing Reiki to the bedroom.

You can do this exercise anywhere you are when you think about it. Ground, Breath, Presence, Creative Power, Send Energy to a focused location on the body. Let's practice so you really get how the energy feels. It is different for everyone, but I guarantee you will feel the difference if you are still and grounded.

After you have done the grounding meditation, hold out your hands facing each other like you are about to clap. Also known as namaste prayer hands. Clap them together once and rub them to create warmth and energy flow. The friction here starts to call the attention you desire to focus your energy flow to. Now that you have created the focus and warmth move them apart yet close enough you barely touch your lingam. Then with intention and concentration to build energy between your hands so you can feel it move them apart. Then back together, then back apart, and repeat. This will look like a slow clap, but you don't touch the palms together. You are waking up the power of your hands and touch. This will also be use in the next chapter. For a minute do this then stop moving and freeze with your hands apart.

Check how much energy you built. Using a little physical movement, test if you feel a full or pulling sensation between your palms.

If you feel the energy between your palms and you are in a private location then bring your energy hands to either side of your lingam without touching it. Hold the intention of the energy being full of life force and vitality mixed with the unconditional love and respect for this sacred wand of light. To give extra healing and compassion to your wand imagine that you have a ball of rose-pink light that you are bathing your sex in. While you are holding this energy over your phallus, breathe up the earth's energy to the head and on the exhale, breathe down the energy from the stars through the top energy center at your crown down into the earth through your body.

Last step in this Lingam Energy Connection meditation. With your hands hovering on either side of your wand and the ball of rose-pink light dripping over your energetic bank of creation and bliss, I want you to connect your energy hands over your wand, your roots in the earth, and now pump your PC/perineum as you draw a deep breath up to your brain. While you draw this breath up, I want you to imagine in your mind's eye, your third eye, your pineal gland, the eye of Ra at the center of your brain where DMT (N-dimethyltryptamine) is produced for the psychotropic experiences of ecstasy, journeys, and pleasure, the most amazing goddess or god, whichever you prefer, is finding a seat energetically on your beautiful glowing light beaming from you lingam. They wrap their warm, juicy body slowly on top of your gland. And while you may have a beautiful gentle "soft on" or a hard-fiery firm "hard-on" either works just fine for this guided meditation.

Now rock your pelvis forward, imagining your wand sliding ever so slowly deeper inside your sexy muse with a deep inhale. Contract and pull up the PC muscles and the sphincter, squeezing all the spinal fluid up the spine to the pineal gland.

When you have squeezed and drawn the juice and energy up to the brain now it is time to release with an exhale and sound that represents the surrender and relaxation this bliss journey is taking you on. And curve your pelvis back to open and release the contraction.

Do this exercise as often as you want to awaken the sleeping giant. Make sure to do this exercise at least one time a day. It should only take you about five to ten minutes. Do about thirty breath cycles. You can do this anywhere you feel comfortable. I often times do it while driving or stopped at a stop sign.

This is your first sensual meditation that we are going to build on later. Enjoy and make a quick entry in your journal to record your experience to see if you have a pattern that you notice.

Share with an accountability partner to make it real in the world.

That last exercise is prepping us for the creation phases. Practice being affectionately detached from any kind of goal orientation. This is an exploratory or experimental exercise to get data points but no need to do anything other than play, observe, and report to an accountability partner what you are getting from the daily practice.

Journal Entry

Please note your findings in you journal. It's creation time, so sit with your journal. Let's find the answer to this chapter: How are you going to get through this fast and easy? The answer is inside you. To look outside you would put you at default instead of in creation. This new relationship to your "turn-on" will come from your creation center. You are going to do this during the journey/meditation. I'm so proud of you. You are doing great.

Creative problem solving is an important tool to have available to you at any time. It is what puts you in the driver's seat of whatever you are focused on. When I taught elementary school children creative dramatics, my whole job was to teach them how to be good at creative problem solving. I would give them challenges that they would have to work out in groups. It is truly amazing what we are all capable of if we have a safe, respectful, and trusting container to experiment in. This is also something that is mandatory to have great, mind-blowing S.E.X. for men and women.

Now go to your journal or sketch pad and doodle on the page. Then, write a word that comes to mind without analysis, just write it and release it. You might hear phrases that you will want to write down. Just go with whatever flows from you into the journal. Once you get to an experience of completion of the release, I want you to write the answer to this question: What is my heart's desire? It can be a phrase, a word, or an entry that is longer in length. Each one of you will have your own way to express your heart's desire. This is for you. No one to show or turn it in to. Unless you'd like to be witnessed in community you may keep all of this in your journal.

Exercise 5.1

Once you have your heart's desire written down, take that and do a project. Make a collage or, even better, a mind movie. If you want a short sweet and simple paper version you will grab a blank white piece of paper. This is just like making a picture collage when you were a kid. Just put a collection of images together that represent your heart's desire. You'll also want to get some magazines. Look through the magazines to find images and cut them out. Now this can be as messy or as perfect as you'd like. It is really up to you and how much you'd like to try on releasing your inner creator.

If you'd rather do this digitally, it is easy to do a mind movie on PowerPoint. And it is simple to search google for images using a key word for the kind of image you are looking for. Quick, fun, and fast to throw images into the PowerPoint slide, add some text, and you're done.

The cool part about doing a mind movie is that you can play the slide show every morning when you get up to a special soundtrack you have saved on you music app of choice. The magic of this work is not going to be obvious to you at the first read of this section. But again, I'm going to ask you to just do the exercise as designed with a curious beginner's mind to see what you may find hidden in the folds of the creation activity. If you have any question about how to create mind movies you can search it online.

The mind, body, spirit connection we weave together, like the Japanese kintsugi, with some healing golden threads constructs a new you, a you that steps every day into your heart's desire. If you think about it, this is exactly the process any of us would do if we were going to create a product for the marketplace.

First, you imagine it in your mind's eye. You can see it. You can watch it act in a scene. You play the movie of your creation over and over again, trying to work it out consciously, and your subconscious mind is also working on it. The mind movie and collages work magic on the subconscious without you doing any hard work. Wow look at that. We are already meeting our goal. I love it.

Here is a link to mind movie examples (www.itshardbook.com/mindmovie) from my life. As a matter of fact, my first step in becoming an author was to create a mind movie for my heart's desire to make this lifelong dream of becoming an author a reality. It was fun, creative, and really helpful to focus daily on moving forward with my book once and for all.

If you would be so bold to post your mind movie or a photo of your heart's desire collage on our community Facebook page, we would all like to celebrate your heart's desire and witness you. Great work, and thank you for doing the work. Now, all you do is watch or look at it every morning when you get up and start your day, and say good night and a gratitude acknowledgement at the end of the day for the magic your heart's desire has already sent your way. This is now going to be your beacon, the lighthouse to guide you when the fog is too thick to see. This is the future you've always wanted to create.

Wounds are the first pitfall to learn how to stay clear of – the one no one sees as a pitfall. We are blinded by wounds. We think they are what we need to do something about. But actually, they are the indicators to practice whole and complete.

Recap of Steps

- Creation (create as you sit in the fog).
- Creative problem solving, discover solutions as you try to create for a purpose.
- Set the beacon of light to show you the way when the fog is too thick. This should be your dream come true/ heart's delight/ goal/ future you.
- Mind movies/ collages.
- Stay the course.
- If the course looks like there is no way through, ask for help until you can keep going forward.
- You are not in this alone. Look around and make a list of all those who are here with you.
- Breathe life into your creation every day.
- Assemble the pieces in your mind's eye.

Chapter 6

OH MY GOD...PLEASE DO THAT AGAIN!

The Power of a S.E.X. M.A.G.I.C. Meditation Session

Frank came to me to get sensual connection because he and his wife hadn't had sex since his son's birth three years earlier, and she asked him to open the relationship to other sexual partners. He was a thirty-six-year-old design engineer who created and invented web experiences for Silicon Valley innovation companies.

Once they agreed, she took a lover, but Frank hadn't gotten any yesses to his requests from other women. He was feeling lonely and hurt by the loss of intimacy with his wife. Later on, it became clear that he was also angry. It turns out when I did his intake, he really resonated with the shamanic approach I brought to the session.

He was also shy to share that he wasn't sure if he had a desirable lingam. He questioned if his size would attract and satisfy a partner. In many ways, he wasn't sure if his stuff worked anymore with a woman because it had been so shut down in his marriage.

I connected with all he shared in the intake and gave him deep empathy for his sorrow, loneliness, and loss. He quickly felt safe and allowed himself to surrender to me and the guidance I provided in the session. It was clear that this man needed to be held in unconditional acceptance. He needed his heart chakra to be held in honor to be able to trust a woman again. I took it slow.

We started with the grounding meditation, taking the first ten minutes to get both of us grounded and connected to the earth's energy. At the end of the meditation, we called in the universe to bring us downloads mixed with stardust into the seventh chakra all the way through the chakras and body into the earth. During this meditation I also introduced the spinal chakra breathing. I could see that this really grounded him so he could receive and go deep. It was time for him to get what he needed – his birthright to have pleasure.

I went to work connecting his brain to his body with all the different elements represented in my touches. He became emotional quickly as I touched him with light brushes of my hair from his feet to his head. We mirrored each other's sounds and went even deeper. As I spread the warm oil all over his back, I grounded him even more with my hands and finished it up with a full body hug to his backside chakras. Here I stayed in stillness for several minutes as he drank in all my chakras' love. He melted and I could feel his body, mind, and spirit give a physical confirmation to my earlier evaluation that he had a deep need to be held by the divine feminine.

When I turned him over, we sat eye gazing for several minutes while I connected his second and fourth chakras. As we gazed, I coached him on breathing and drawing his energy up through his chakras and out of the top of his head. I asked him if I could hold his lingam and, with his permission, I held him while I said a blessing and prayer that acknowledged all that he went through and all his gifts to the world. He was moved to tears and I could see how badly he needed his heart to be healed from the grief and loss of his marriage. He took another deep breath, drawing the sensation of gratitude and love into every cell in his body, and just like that he got a world of healing. But this was just the beginning and I had more in store for him to receive from the goddess.

I did deep lingam and perineum tension release work before offering a prostate massage. He agreed to let me work his base chakra. During the prostate massage, he went deep into pleasure mixed with moments of his sadness for all he put into his marriage without feeling like his own needs were met. I kept working the places where there were emotions coming up and had him breathe the energy up his spine with an "Ah" sound and pull the energy up the body squeezing one set of muscles after another from the base of the spine to the top of the head and out. He felt held and loved and witnessed for the first time.

Since this first session, Frank has come to see me four times. His relationship ended in a divorce and I'm still working with him to move through his relationship transition and find pleasure all areas of his life.

Your partner's role in helping you is an important component to your healing. But first you must get a strong enough willpower to not get kicked off center. Please continue to do your personal work and we will add in your partner by teaching you how to put your awareness over on your partner, which also helps you. I recommend that partners plan for their intimacy time. This doesn't sound sexy, but trust me, if you put it on the calendar and keep your appointments with your partner it will create a sense of trust, respect and safety that opens partners to deeper connection and love.

Your role in helping yourself is going to be revealed slowly as you walk the path and practice what you've learned. I would like you to be sensual with yourself at least five minutes a day. That's not so much time to where it would be a problem. I love doing solo sexual meditations, as well as coupled sexual meditations.

Enjoy the soft on. If I can teach you nothing else about sexual satisfaction without hard work it is this: That which you resist persists. In other words, if you can be okay with what is in any given moment, the situation will pass on its own or disappear completely. There is no need to push or force something to happen. If you give it space and allow it to be exactly the way it is and exactly the way it isn't, it will find a resolution or disappear. When we resist something and show no acceptance is when it gets all sticky on us. In other words, when we resist what is happening in our life it's like pushing piles of dirt around from place to place thinking that is getting rid of it. But it just makes a bigger mess that you have to clean up later, adding to the upset.

Exercise 6.0

Breathe desire up from the earth. Be willing to have desire stir inside you and grow. If it is not growing, you must look at what is stopping you from putting energy there. Energy, sex, and what is possible is beyond what we can persevere. Without the profound experience of energetic embodied ecstasy it is impossible to level up our consciousness. Which is why I feel that regular sensual play and exploration will fire up your wand the more you do it. Rewire the neurobiology of your body's manifestation of pleasure/hard-on.

Have sex as often as you wish or when works for you and your partner. Remember you are an autonomous being that has a right to have your own pleasure. No one is the head human who gets to say what that is for you. And all of us must be responsible with any contracts we have with the people in our lives in the form of wedding vows.

Tantra weave it all together with your current skills.

The time has finally come. We will dive into tantra yoga for the embodiment of sensual connection and sacred experiences of xstasy. Strap in and hang on, as it is a jam-packed lesson to devour.

There are many definitions of tantra yoga on the web. Here is one from Yogajournal.com that will help us understand what the practice is.

"The word tantra means to weave or expand. The idea with tantra yoga, then, is to weave together many yoga practices, and other spiritual styles and teachings, in order to connect with others and the universe. Tantra yoga is a type of yoga that employs various rituals to study the universe through the human microcosm. While most of us think of sex when we think of Tantra Yoga, this ancient practice is actually a powerful combination of asana, mantra, mudra, and bandha (energy lock) and chakra (energy center) work that you can use to build strength, clarity, and bliss in everyday life. By harnessing and embodying the five forces of Shakti, the female deity that represents creativity and change, Tantric Yoga suggests we can move through the world with more confidence and contentment."

When many of us search for answers to challenges we have in our lives, we often look for those answers in a place that doesn't work to find new, out-of-your-box ideas. This is because we are blind to an aspect of the process of creation. If you think about the creation story, it starts with the abyss; first there was everything and nothing, all at once. Then, in order for source to experience itself it separated and polarized so it could know itself in that expression of source at that moment. Tantra yoga is a way of dancing in this cosmic swing to practice what is your innate function, to be a creator, made in the image of the creator. Your job in this life is to master creation in all the ways that you can so you will know yourself as a being who can imagine and manifest what your heart's desire and to support your life purpose.

S.E.X. M.A.G.I.C. Meditation Format

Step M: Meet and Greet Welcome Ritual

Welcomes are important to putting partners at ease in your presence. When you honor a person's entrance into an experience, you set the tone for how the experience is going to go for them. Depending on how you welcome them, you will tell them what to expect. I don't want you to feel pressure over this. I want it to settle your own nerves to know that if you put a little reverence into welcoming your partner, however you do that, it will be the perfect container to make them feel held in a safe space.

When a person, man or woman, feels safe, they can surrender into courageous vulnerability and the abyss of ecstasy beyond anything you can conceive of. The process of opening up is possible when we feel held. Every person needs something different to feel this way. You will need to become incredibly curious and interested in the other person. Listen. Say, "thank you, anything else?" until they have nothing else to say. And be able to reflect to them what you think you heard them say so they feel heard, understood, and valued.

In the beginning of our Sacred Experience of Xstasy (S.E.X.) Meditation, take a moment where both of you drop into each other's worlds and check in. This is a time to share what your day has been like. If there was anything that has happened today that is stuck in your space or mind, or holding you up in anyway. This can also be seen as a clearing conversation to prepare the person or people to let go of anything that would get in the way of them connecting from a place of being whole and complete in that moment. As a tantra practitioner this is what I call an intake interview for that session. I do this for every session even if I've already had 100 sessions with that person.

The is not a time for long stories that go on and on about things that have no end in sight. This part should really only take about ten to fifteen minutes or less. Feel free to ask your partner if it is okay to redirect them to simple "what is so" kinds of answers. What is so is only the facts, not the story you are telling yourself about the facts. This will support them to get right to the point. Most people can't tell when they are going into story to avoid or protect themselves from being hurt in intimacy.

Intimacy can be seen as In-To-Me-See. If someone feels like being seen is unsafe, they will dance a convincing spectacle to divert your ability to see them. If you do this well you will make a huge difference in another person's life for the better. What I have found is, people love to be truly seen exactly the way they are and exactly the way they aren't. In other words, people want to be "gotten." This is what we all look for in a relationship. To be accepted, heard, understood, and valued – gotten. When you experience being gotten in this way, you will want to do this for others and return to the space that person held for you over and over again.

You may even find that this is a huge turn-on. It takes courageous vulnerability to be received and welcomed in this way. But when you go there and your nervous system is truly settled, feeling whole and complete, your body's autonomic nervous system will do exactly what it is supposed to do: Grow and reproduce more of that experience. In other words, you will get hard and aroused, and so will your partner.

But you can't have getting hard as a goal or an in-order-to kind of transaction. This goal orientation will kill your orgasm and hard-on. The nervous system of a human being can smell that miles away. Don't try to do it or hide it because it won't work. The nerves will be able to tell, even if they don't know that they are smelling a goal orientation. You will see them protect themselves or weasel out of the situation somehow. Stay present and curious about them and they will guide you by the dance they are doing.

Here are some questions you can ask in the welcome stage:

Is there anything that isn't working in your life right now that you would like to let go of?

Do you feel incomplete about anything that if it was complete you would be able to let go?

What would you like to use this session to create for your life?

Is there anything missing that if it was here would make all the difference for you and your life?

Step A: Away Clear The Past Water Purification Ritual

We move into a sacred communion with the element of water now to purify your mind, body, and spirit of any final remaining thoughts, physical cleanliness, and disturbances in your field. Water is a feminine energy and sets the stage for you to be cleared of anything that doesn't serve the meditation.

Since the meditation will be intimate, this is a time to use the water to clean all your most sacred parts, even your base chakra, also known as your buttocks, crack, anus, rectum, foreskin, feet, toes, ears, nose, mouth, armpits, and any area you want your partner to visit during the session. When you feel fresh and clean physically, you will be more open to being seen and touched and even tasted.

I'm not suggesting that you become a clean freak or fearful of getting sick, but what I do believe in is being tasty for your partner, whatever that is for them. I know of some people who love the smell of different body parts. The point here is to create an experience that will make your partner want to devour you and you them. This is definitely a H.A.R.D. conversation opportunity to ask your partner what he or she likes, and for you to share what you like.

H.A.R.D. Conversations

Having the talk that you are afraid to have but that you know will not go away if you ignore it.

Acknowledge how vulnerable it is for you to address the issue.

Respect them more than hiding in fear or upset.

Demonstrate courage by being the kind of person who faces the hard conversations.

When you or your partner go to bathe, remember that this is a time to let go of anything that doesn't serve you any longer. Let the water wash away and purify your mind, body and spirit that would get in the way of your sacred experience of ecstasy. You may want to have this water purification ritual in a shower, bath, waterfall, wash bin, or any creative way that turns you and your partner on. Have fun with this and be sexy and of service to the sacred process of letting go.

Step G: Go Into the Grounded Space

Once you and your partner's purification is complete then we meet on a massage table or bed that has been preset to be a warm, comfortable nest to receive the blessing of the meditation. This grounding meditation, or ritual, is an integral part of the process. If you do nothing else before you do this meditation, please do this.

I always tell my clients that if I didn't do this with them it would be like sending a kite into the sky without a string. The kite would fly, but it would also crash and burn and probably not survive the experience to try it again later. The grounding is like the string that tethers you to the earth and allows you to go even higher than you've ever gone. It also allows you to do an amazing sky dance, performing amazing aerial tricks and amazing yourself.

Step I: Intimate Touch and Brain Connection Ritual

You are now ready to be the giver and the receiver. When you schedule this meditation with your partner, decide who will be the giver and who will be the receiver. The more you can keep all negotiations out of the session room, the better for keeping the space safe for each person to stay in their roles for the experience. In other words, keep business out of the sensual space. Do all of that when setting up the session so sexy, flowing feminine and strong and supportive masculine can show up.

Whether you do this as a self-honoring practice (masturbation) or a partnered meditation, you increase your own sexual energy. Hold an increase in your sexual energy by pumping your PC muscles and pulling the energy up your body. Move with flow and rhythm to keep it going.

This is all about touch and tantalizing the body so the brain can lay down as many neurological pathway as possible. Pet your partner with five different kinds of touch. Earth, Water, Air, Fire, Ether.

Sharpen the Knife Stroke to Increase Circulation and Ejaculation control (Mantak Chia Taoist Practice)

Warm coconut oil in hands.

Cup your lingam and testicles in warm oiled hands.

Say an intention, prayer, or mantra to show reverence for the sleeping giant to awaken and embody the pleasure or desire and turn-on.

Hold the base of your shaft with your non-dominant hand and squeeze as if you are holding a straw up toward your face. This will prevent the blood flow from going out the wand. If it feels like you don't have the right hold or spot, keep practicing to find the perfect spot for you. With practice you will start to see what works best for you.

With your dominant hand, squeeze and pull the blood flow and energy and pleasure up the shaft to the head/gland. Pull this stroke fifty times up. Pause if you get close to the point of no return. Do the breathing technique that smooths out the climax. The grounding breath is what to use here. Other than this, just keep stroking to exercise your lingam to get the result you want. Do fifty strokes pointed up, then point down toward the feet, now point to right leg, last point to the left leg, all fifty strokes.

When you get close to the point of no return pause and breathe the energy of the climax the opposite direction of the squirt. You draw up the inside of the body to the center of your creation machine, which is the pineal gland. This lights up and fuels this gland with the creation energy of the sex organs and creation center of the body. I don't want you to ejaculate during this process. I want you to practice bringing yourself to the point of no return and separate orgasm from ejaculation.

In modern sex practices most people believe that men can only have one orgasm at a time. Because what Western lovers are used to is a man ejaculating and collapsing into a zombie state. The assumption is that ejaculation is the only way a man can orgasm. The reason men go catatonic after ejaculation is due to how a man's body creates the ejaculate. When a man contributes his seed to a woman's body to create a baby the seed needs to be embodied with all the energy a man can spare to give his offspring the best chance of surviving. The man's body takes the energy from each organ and deposits the life force and sperm into the ejaculate to be safely delivered into his woman's womb. This leaves a man depleted as if he just ran a marathon. If you have ever run a marathon you know it is exhausting and requires a least a day to recover from the initial deple-tion. Most people wouldn't think to go run a marathon in another hour or even a day. But this is what you are doing if you ejaculate day after day.

If you are not making a baby you are sending your valuable life force energy out of your body. Instead of squirting that energy out, follow the age rules below for how long you should refrain from releasing this energy. On the days you are recovering from your previous ejaculation you will get to the point before the point of no return, pause and breathe the orgasmic sensation and energy up the spine to the top of your head and wash your brain, impregnating yourself with creative energy. You will feel high and electric. There is a better way. For men with impotence and ED you need to keep this important energy to rebuild the energy that has been lost for however long you have had a lack of erections.

You might feel lightheaded and your body will have contractions in your sex and maybe even throughout your body. The more you allow and relax into it the bigger and longer the non-ejaculatory orgasm will be.

Follow the age rule for how often you should be ejaculating for your age.

Taoist Ejaculation Control Guidelines:
- Twenty years or less hold off ejaculating four days
- Thirty years or less hold off eight days
- Forty years or less hold off two weeks
- Fifty years or less hold off three weeks
- Sixty years on up hold off four weeks at a time

You may have as much sex and masturbate as much as you would like. Just breathe all the energy up the body every time and see how alive you start to feel. This will give you multiple orgasms and break the habit of ejaculation only orgasm. Breathing up the energy allows the body to expand the container to enjoy the experience of bliss.

If you cum by doing any part of this exercise, please celebrate – honor what your body has done. This will positively anchor the gratitude with the physical result.

Next, pulse the PC muscle and the prostate gland. With the pulse you are going to visualize and imagine the fluid pulled up the spine to the brain. Feel this pleasure all the way up. Have an orgasm in the brain.

Rinse and repeat. Do as often you wish with or without a partner.

Once you have completed this, with or without ejaculation, go to Step C.

Step C: Corpse Pose and Close Session: Shavasana Mantra Ritual

Shavasana or Corpse Pose, is a pose in yoga used to rest and integrate what lessons have been receive from the day's practice.

As your partner is melting into the relaxation this is when you reaffirm the intentions and creation set at the beginning of the session. To be in shavasana is to surrender to the integration of the work done in the session that will continue for years to come. It is the most important part of the whole session. It's when the energy takes form in your body. Stillness is the only action you both should take at this moment.

This is a time for autonomy and to just be in stillness with nowhere to go, nothing to do but breathe and receive the gifts of the session and the sacred reverence that was shown to your mind, body, and soul. It is powerful and profound.

Chapter 7

HOW DO I ASK SO I GET THE CLIMAX I WANT?

This could be a book all on its own. There are aspects to this in relationships that I'm not going to be able to give deep explanations for in this book, but I expand on and work with students in my workshops in depth. Here is a brief overview of what will help you get started.

To truly communicate your needs and desires in a way that works for both masculine and feminine friendly styles you must put yourself over in the shoes or views or filters you will be speaking into. This is why books like *Men Are from Mars, Women Are from Venus* have been so helpful and healing to relationships because they shed light on how the other person might see the world. In my programs we work a lot on the dynamics at play with the sexes.

Once you can hear how the other side is experiencing interactions with you, you may notice that there are some areas that may need to be cleaned up from past upsets. Use my H.A.R.D. conversations system to clean this up is recommended. Practice on little things to start so it is less triggering and gentler on all involved. If you need support join our coaching calls that I do to support you through these practices. Practice and master the clean-up process so when you accidently step in it, you can clean it up faster and faster with ease and grace instead of old tactics for protecting yourself from the consequences of doing something that doesn't work.

Masculine/Feminine dynamics are very important but again a whole other book. Please consider that all relationships have exchange of energy. Negotiate before you install the energy or the energy will be used for something other than what the agreement and both with be chasing it. When you get in to a relationship you evaluate the cost and benefits to having the relationship in your life. Most of us hope that we get just as much if not more than what we put in. The concept of price of admission is one that relationship columnist Dan Savage has coined.

To give you a little view into this idea imagine your partner is a slave to a job. Slaves are owned and have to do what the master says. She is not free to be with you when she is at said job. She must complete that to get her mind, body and spirit off that so she can focus on you. As her partner, if you want her to focus on you and not other things, your job is to find a way to meet the need the job fills for her.

If the job provides the ability to drive her children to school so they can get an education and be free, then find a way to support her getting that result. If you can't do it.

Find someone who can. If a woman has a need that isn't getting met she will have a percent of energy dedicated to that need getting met and not to you. The crazy thing is that most of us have hundreds of needs not getting met which are keeping us from being truly present for deep love and connection. Do anything you can to get all needs handled so you and your lover can have deep love and connection.

You've heard people say, "I wasn't born with an instruction manual." Not that anyone would read it, except for the engineers in the room. Well, I was raised by an engineer so I picked up on some things from being raised in constant problem solving mode with my dad. If my sister and I weren't helping to build a fence or assisting him in sawing plywood with the table saw to build kitchen cabinets, we were driving a tractor or "using our common sense," in my dad's words, so he didn't have to come help us do our jobs.

We kids, at early ages, had to know how to handle whatever came our way.

As part of this kind of family upbringing, my parents were open with their relationship communication styles. They fought in front of us, they made up in front of us, they even showed affection and publicly appropriate intimacy that we kids could read as Mom and Dad loving each other. They were courageous young parents raising us on principles that they aligned with each other on. One of the principles was to have open communications around sex and relationships. I gathered from the stories they shared (and the fact that I am a child of the seventies and California had the free love movement) that the topic was not something that they would shy away from. At the age of thirteen, there I was on a long family road trip in the motorhome and Mom and Dad decided to ask my sister and me if we were going to save ourselves for marriage. Well, my older sister Julie answered first with, "Of course I am. It is my big plan to save myself for that special time after my wedding." As my sister answered, I prepared for the moment when the interrogation would turn to me. What would I say? Could I say what I really wanted to say, or should I be safe and just copy her? As I crafted what to say, my sister who is thirteen months older than me, finished and they all stared at me. I took a deep breath and went for it.

"Well," my little thirteen-year-old self said, "I'm actually not sure if I'll ever make it to the wedding day and this seems like a really important thing to miss out on. I want to have sex before I get married, because I want to make sure to know what it feels like in case I die before I get married."

"Hmm" is the look I got back from all in the motorhome driving down the road. Then, my mom chimed in with, "Well, is this going to be a special person or how are you going to choose the person to do this with?" Now unfortunately I wasn't privileged to know what my mom and dad were actually thinking, but it was probably something like, "Oh shoot. We didn't see that coming. Or did we?"

As a mother myself, I imagine that would have been scarring to hear come from my daughter at thirteen. The conversation turned out to be one of the most important conversations of my life. It showed me that in the area of intimacy and sex, it is really important to talk about it with your family and understand how to be the best member of your family you can be. This was clearly an important milestone in my life's purpose.

Why did I share all of this with you? Well, I wanted to give you a sense of how really sensitive communications can go to support your own steps in this direction. In this chapter, you will learn ways to communicate in sensitive and challenging moments to bring the necessary healing and support for you as you move through the *It's HARD* process.

Were you taught from an early age how to communicate during sex? Probably not how to talk about sex but rather how not to talk about sex. As we discussed at the beginning of the chapter, none of us were given an instruction manual. You are perfectly normal. I really want you to get that. You are normal if you didn't have a crazy family like mine who talked about our sex goals as we drove down the freeway in the old Winnebago.

Now that you know you are normal, I want you to see that there is a range you probably fall somewhere in between the areas of no communication at all or an excess of communication. Wherever you find yourself is where we start. In earlier chapters I introduced the concept of the ROS and SOS. You have been working on noticing any patterns and beliefs and communication styles you have. It is important to keep a simple journal where you use handwriting to record these SOS patterns and the ways your system works and doesn't work for you. By now you will have picked up on things that maybe you will want to make adjustments for. This is a perfect place to be.

Step 1: Notice How You Operate in Communication.

Some questions you might ask are, "Am I comfortable talking about sex with my partner, my parents, my friends, myself, my (fill in the blank)?" And really look here. This is a time to be clear and straight with yourself. It's okay, it's just you and me and we get to talk openly about how this is for you. I am your temporary accountability sharing partner who will get you to a comfortable state in this new area, kind of like communication training wheels that you get to take off once you get the hang of it. Get *real* with yourself. Write it down and it will free you from the constraints it has over you. Notice how in the story above I had to first get straight with myself about the question my mom and dad had for me. Only then could I have the courage to speak my truth about the question they asked.

Step 2: Understand Needs and How Needs Communicate

Why are needs the important next step? Well, here's the thing about needs, every one of us has seven core human needs.

1. Certainty
2. Variety/Creativity/Uncertainty
3. Significance/Being Important
4. Intimacy/Love/Connection
5. Contribution/Sharing/Making a Difference
6. Growth and Development
7. Spirituality

But each of us has our own cocktail of priority and order that is unique to us. And you will also find if you look back at your life through this lens that you will have a different percentage of importance in your life. Why is that important? Let's say Sally and Harry were married and Sally really needed significance to be one priority in her life with Harry. But Harry knew nothing about needs because he grew up in a family where the culture didn't allow sex to be discussed. Sally tries to hint at what she needs, but Sally was also not raised to communicate, but instead was told that her job as a kid was to be seen not heard, so she doesn't talk much about anything challenging. But every day when Harry gets home he doesn't make a point to come greet her. He just quietly comes in and seemingly ignores her. He thinks, "Wow I'm an amazing husband. I have a quiet wife and out of respect I'm not going to disturb her." And she thinks, "Why am I not important to my husband? He comes home and just ignores me." This is what we humans do in the name of relating. What I've found working with couples is that when you can see you have a need in the relationship that is not getting met, recognizing that is generally going to free you up to ask for what you need. And if that person isn't willing to or interested in doing that, you have to find another way to get that need met.

Chapter 8

THANK GODDESS!

Gratitude, one of the most important actions to take every day. Growing up, I would see the Christian prayer hands in picture form on the walls. I always wondered what that meant. Now that I'm forty-eight, I have a deep appreciation of the gratitude of prayer.

When I first studied tantra with Master Charles Muir. I had the first session with one of the advanced practitioners. I was quite nervous to go into it because I had no idea what was going to happen. But I knew I wanted to be grateful for what my body did to get me to this point in my life. After all, it gave me my baby girl, Sydney, and the amazing experiences of orgasm and being a first-place long distance runner. And making a goal with my head from a field goal kick in a tournament in Hawaii for a traveling soccer team when I was the last and youngest player to be added to the roster. Let's just put it this way: This body of mine rocks and I'm so grateful for it.

But it wasn't always that way. There were times when I wanted to cut off parts of it because it was too hard to deal with. There were times when it felt like it betrayed me, like when I lost four babies. But I have reverence for those experiences now because of all that they gave me in the lessons of my life. I'm on the other side of the struggles of my past. I can't tell you for sure if my Lyme disease will show its ugly head again but I'm not running from it. I'm actually empowered by it because I will not be paying any energy to it and therefore I'm free from the hold it could have on me.

This is when you transmute the pain and suffering of anything in life to be the superpower you had all along. You just need to be the sculptor who chisels away the stone that doesn't belong to the sculpture. If I look back at my life, I have had more hero's journeys or branches to my journey than I wish upon anyone. But I would not change any of them to all the gold in the world. If I hadn't gone through those things, I would not been the whole person I am today: The kind of person who can trust herself to be there when I say I will be there. Complete a project when I say I will. Or give a vow or commitment to a partner. Yes, this is what all the hard work is for.

You are this perfect ten of a person that everyone wants to be with and should be labeled the sexiest man alive for whatever magazine that is. That would be interesting, but really at the bottom of a lifetime of work we are all wanting to the person we could be proud of. I'm proud of you. I know how hard this problem has been for you. I've been there. I don't have a lingam, but that is okay. I see the look in the eyes of men I work with who are heartbroken that their virility does not work. As if they had lost the one thing that made life worth living. Life is hard and it feels good to have pleasure. We are pleasure animals that need connection and love, and one of the ways we do that is with our erogenous zones and reproductive organs – which are also our creation energy centers –and by communication of our desire to relate one on one.

Why gratitude? And why Thank Goddess? Well that is simple. A way for you to be up to something bigger than yourself. You have to have focus outside of yourself to do that, so if that is true, then giving reverence or gratitude to the divine goddess would bring yummy energy to your divine masculine. And that is an important part of the cycle of arousal. See, most of us grew up thinking that it was the pictures we saw in the magazine or in pornography that got us hard or turned on, but actually it was a desire to be a part of each other. Like a magnet that just won't stay away for another, the dance of the masculine–feminine has the law of polarities working in its favor. What does that have to do with gratitude? When you honor something and hold it as precious you acknowledge all things, because you can't have reverence for the divine feminine and not for yourself and the divine masculine too. If you are a man in a relationship with a woman or any order of male or masculine identifying person, having reverence for the feminine, whether that is your girlfriend or boyfriend or other partner, brings you into balance and wholeness.

Here is the process you can practice to have gratitude and reverence every day:

1. Start with a gratitude journal. Use whatever journal you have, or pick one for this purpose alone. I often have multiple journals going at once. Do it however you want. The most important part about this is that you hand write a gratitude every day. It could be in the morning or evening, but take as little as five minutes to sit in silence and get present to at least one thing you are grateful for.

2. Next, as you get better at expressing gratitude to yourself, you are going to pick one random person a day to express gratitude for or reverence for. This is an opportunity to see the results in others from expressing gratitude and reverence. At this step, which will be seven days after Step 1, you will have results to record in your journal of the expressed gratitude you shared today. This is part of your reprograming your SOS/ROS to include acknowledgement as power. When we have gratitude for things it sets or goes deeper into the nervous system and supports your autonomic nervous responses to experiences in life. Have more gratitude for any area of life and you will start to see life turns you on.

3. Now when you have something you are grateful for pump you PC muscles three time or more. "What? Why would you say to do that?" Well you are teaching your body to be turned on by things you appreciate. This is bio-hacking and neuro-linguistic programming (NLP) and laying down new neurological pathways to be alive and turned on by life. Now I'm not asking you

to show anyone that you are doing this. I'm asking you to simply internally contract your muscle at the base of your torso, the PC, or pubococcygeus muscle or taint or perineum, is the muscle that helps you start and stop urine. You are doing this for many reasons. *None* of which is to be lewd or offensive. You are simply connecting gratitude to your second chakra, or laying the wires energetically from your gratitude brain centers down your body to your base bottom of spin.

But here is how you are going to start to apply this all in the bedroom. Looking back at the chapter about S.E.X., you have a ritual to set up the room and space like a nest to show a level of reverence for your lover that is sacred. When she is greeted this way, this meets important needs for anyone but especially for a woman who considers opening her most sacred of all places on her body. If she doesn't treat or know her body in that way, you will template that for her to see that her body is to be honored and so are her choices as to how to respect herself.

Guys, for many of the women in your lives you will be the man who stands for that woman to be worshiped. If not you, then who? Do you really want her going somewhere else to get the need filled? No, let me just answer that for you right now. You want her to trust that when she is with you, she can count on you honoring and holding her as divine. If you do that for her, you will be amazed at how she shows you she reveres you and your favorite buddy. That's right, we woman actually love loving up our guys. (Don't worry my book for women will be out next and I'll teach them all they need to know to revere you.) See, when a woman is deep in gratitude and worshiping her man, she will naturally want you to feel good and share how good it feels to be turned on by that and the cycle then goes into you and you'll have the kind of love loop we want in this dance.

The techniques I teach you about working on your own body and how your body works can and should be practiced with a partner (female or male) so you can see how it all works on someone else. You must practice them on yourself and on a partner to get good at it but to also learn from experience. The more you do it, the more energy you can feel and the better your erection will get.

Even if all you did was do a S.E.X. magic session on your partner and not on yourself, or if your partner is the receiver every time and you are the giver, you will increase the blood flow in your lingam and strengthen your erection.

The act of being of service to another person requires you to create the same energy you encourage the other person to have. That means that in order for you to be the space of increased sexual energy for your partner you have to generate that in yourself. And because you are doing it for another person your focus will be being of service and your autonomic nervous system will take over and your erection will show up again.

At first it will tingle. Then it will surprise you with a fullness. And before you know it you'll be turned on and hard at the thought of giving to your partner again and again. You may even start to be the one putting the sessions on the calendar.

Do You Know How To Make A Cat Purr?

You pet it the way it wants to be petted. If the cat doesn't like the way you pet it, it will let you know by getting away from you, hissing at you, or biting and scratching you to get you away from it.

What does this sound like, gentlemen? Yes, that's right, women do all of these things in different ways. Your job is to not react to women's behavior as how dare this woman react that way to me.

Look at her actions as communicating in a language you will get the decoder for in this book. Women and feminine energy (the molecule and the atom, in comparison) are easy to understand once you know what you are looking at. To do this, you must have a curious mind. The more curious you become, the more wonder you will see in the world.

This reminds me of a moment in my life when I experienced knowing the distinction wonderment. My divorce started a month earlier. I was trying to figure out how to survive. I was in a car accident two months before resulting in a bad head injury. All this while running a high-end, eco-friendly toy store and art studio. Raising an eight-year-old. Managing employees to work the store so I could be home with my daughter.

It didn't feel as if it was going so well in any area of my life. I felt as if I was a raging witch. The Hindu have a goddess who fits these characteristics. Her name is Kali. I was definitely Kali in that time.

I was in so much pain. I was angry at the universe for not giving me a break. One day I lashed out on Facebook and said, "I'm so frustrated... I need to find a class that I can take to learn how to be a strong, powerful, business-woman without being a witch."

Within thirty minutes, my dear friend Jim chimed in and said simply, "I do, and it's happening this weekend in San Francisco." It was the transformation course called the Landmark Forum and Jim and I reviewed it with about 350 other graduates of the program.

The woman leading the course was amazing. One day, she brought up the idea of being curious. Curious about everything. Be curious just to be curious. That night we were sent home with homework and instructions to go to a curious dinner with classmates.

Well, with all the things I listed that I was dealing with, including infertility, three babies lost, sexual frustration and Lyme disease, I had become one of the most serious, significant, and angry woman that ran a creative, playful, and whimsical toy store and art studio you'd ever seen. When she got me to be curious I realized how hard I had become. I was rigid. I didn't like myself or how I had come to survive the challenges I had had in my life. In a moment of curiosity of why that was I considered my job. A job I created from nothing and was my dream. In that moment I realized that I was a "Toy Store Owner," of one of the coolest toy stores I have ever seen and it was full of love and healthy toy choices to make families' lives safe to play. My passion was creating opportunities for people to love the experience of life.

It was absurd. I was a toy store owner. I had the perfect job to play and have fun all day long with my employees, customers, local business owners, events, and projects. It could be naturally playful like the kids and my daughter I created it for. Like my drama kids. I created the store because of how playing games changed all of our lives.

I was a new person the second day. I was not recognizable to most people as the dark, angry woman who was there the day before.

While discussing the results of our curiosity experiment the night before, the course leader introduced a term I hadn't remembered learning as part of the curriculum ten years earlier when I first graduated from the course.

She had us contemplate wonderment from the perspective of a three-year-old little girl running through the airport at 6:00 a.m., excited to jump on a plane. Meanwhile, all the early morning passengers were not so enthused. Why was she so vital and alive so early in the morning? Because at that age, she saw everything in the world as new and curious and wonderful.

She was not weighted down by experiences of the past that, instead of being resolved, had sucked energy out of adults after a lifetime of struggle, disappointment, and heartache. She was free, vital, intoxicating, and charming. Everything I had wanted to have in my life.

That's it. I had been missing curious wonderment and I was teaching Open Ended Play and Imagination Awakening at my whimsical fairyland toy store, Treehouse in the Glen.

When I told my employee what breakthrough I had for myself and how I brought playfulness and fun to the workplace, they were all for it. I gave them freedom to show up and express themselves and trust their own imaginations. The side benefit I didn't expect is that I worked less hard than when I was trying hard to struggle through it.

I want to say, as a side note to the list of things that happened to me in my life up to that point, it was not easy. Getting to the freedom I'm describing here, the kind of awakening I'm guiding you to with every secret in this book, any one of those things on the list would be hard to get through. I am not making light of any of them. Every single one was a valley of terror on my hero's journey. If anything, I'm wanting you to see that hard comes in many forms and extremes. Whether you are applying the process in this book to your erectile function or to moments of terror, it works the same to liberate the life force/chi/prana/ and vitality of a three-year-old.

And at the end of this book you will need to be curious about the wonderment of women in order to learn how to make her sing in the bedroom like she is the most beautiful guitar masterfully being stroked by a prodigy. To come full circle to the first session I ever had with Jacob, all he did for me was witness me naked as he placed his hands on/over my pussy/yoni and said a prayer or reverence or honor out loud and also silently. I wept and wept. I felt like a queen who was seen for the first time for all she is at the heart instead of her rugged business-like outer shell.

Often times when I work with someone, I ask them to do little Mr. Miyagi things that might not be a direct connection to the work we were doing but that have a deeper connection to the subconscious mind or the auto-programing of the person's system. Here is an acknowledgement that one of my students wrote in the form of a love letter to me as reflection to what he got out of the day's work we did together.

The Turquoise Temptress
Erik B.

"She greets you at the doorway of your own
consciousness, and invites you to step inside.
'Further inside,' she cries, moaning
your Spirit back into
Presence with
Today.
'You've never known a truer love,'
she reminded. 'Than yourself.'
He paused to reflect
on her words for the
feeling of satiety
was certainly
satisfying.

That is all she wants you to know.
When you speak, she listens.
When you sigh, she knows.
When you forget, she
brings you back
into a higher
state of
Being.

'I can't write a single line,' he sighed.
'That would do her justice.'
'For in her presence,
you feel grounded
and whole. And you
feel it down deep,
way down to
your Soul.'

And her language of the Soul
Is not spoken in words.
She speaks to you
in tongues that
curl across lips
leaving a clear
sweet taste
of Bliss.

A verse in reverence,
To the Eternal One
with a Mending
Heart.

It's little things like this that make a woman open to you in her heart and with her legs. See, when women feel totally taken care of, they relax and open. Oh, and by the way so do you. You want your intimate partner to have the present moment on her mind, which is where the sensation of opening will draw her to you and your juicy, sexy energy that you have been building and responsibly enjoying on your own and in your own energy field. You literally want her to come to you because she can't help herself.

All of us humans have senses the are invisible to us until we unlock the awareness. The exercises I'm giving you in this chapter are how to fill your interactions every day, and most importantly the intimate ones, with spirit and lots and lots of lifeforce energy.

Remember the energy center of the body you put awareness on is the center of creation. The center that produces another human being. To have reverence for this most important of all centers where we were all born from, we have a connection to the Creator/Source/God/Universe. This brings blessings and more growth. And isn't growth what all of us hope is the result of the work we've been doing? I mean, you want your wand to grow and expand, right? Well, what if it was as easy as saying a grateful prayer to your body and that of your partners. And what if that presence is the spark that lets it be okay exactly as your erection is and exactly as your erection isn't? What if you could find the things you love about the way your lingam is?

I had a lover once who learned that most of his life, he worked at controlling his orgasms so he could have sex for longer with women. But now that he was in his fifties, he found that it was harder for him to cum. But here's the beauty that he found on his own: He now can have sex with his partner for as long as she wants. That is a big plus to the partner because she is then in the driver's seat as to how long they go.

In tantra, we teach that a man doesn't need to ejaculate every time. But then how does he orgasm? This is an important thing to remember and learn how to do: a separation of ejaculation and orgasm. When we have this collapsed, we think the man needs to ejaculate in order to have an orgasm or complete the process. But as we discussed in the tantric section, you may draw that energy of orgasm up the body to fuel it and support well-being and expand the energy of the body instead of squirting it out to produce a kid. If you aren't making a baby, why waste the energy?

But what if you orgasm at a time you don't want, or you want the orgasm? You can take the gratitude practice and turn your ejaculation into a Conscious Cum, where you thank the goddess you are with and the divine feminine in her for bringing you this gift of S.E.X. You may want to anoint each one of your energy centers to bring your body back the energy that left through the ejaculate.

In this way, you and your partner stay in reverence and connected as your lovemaking comes to a close. Too many times we just roll over and don't know what to say. This is the most precious moment of a person's day – to have an orgasm witnessed by another. In terms of bio-hacking or

NLP or reprogramming your SOS/ROS, when someone has just had an orgasm, they're in a kind of trance state. Here's where integrity comes in. Now that you are learning this you must use this knowledge for making a difference with your partner. This is not a place you want to use to be negative or destructive to another. Karma is painful and it does come back around for you to learn and clean up. Don't think you can get away with it. The universe knows. In trance is when affirmation and suggestions are the most powerful. When you give an appreciation or acknowledgement or blessing, you program them to be that which you have said that they were in the gratitude statement. You are literally creating them to show up for you the way you have thanked them. Try it and see what the results are. I'm sure you are going to be amazing and surprised at how well this works.

Here is a Hawaiian forgiveness prayer I love to teach my clients to use in any number of situations. It's called Ho'oponopono and below are the steps to take and an explanation.

How to Make Ho'oponopono a Practice for Healing Relationships

- Step 1: Close your eyes and imagine in your mind's eye a person you would like to send this forgiveness prayer to. See their face and gaze into their eyes as if they are standing in front of you. Feel their presence in your heart.

- Step 2: Place your right hand (sending energy hand) on your heart and your left hand (receiving energy hand) on your solar plexus or 3rd chakra, which is below your heart center three finger widths below the sternum.

- Step 3: Put your grounding roots in place by recalling the grounding meditation we practiced earlier.

- Step 4: Take three deep breaths inhaling the earth's energy up your roots into your body, and as you release and exhale, open your crown, or 7th chakra, to receive universal energy into the creation of your prayer of forgiveness and Ho'oponopono while running the visualization in your mind's eye like a mind movie of the prayer being delivered to this person's being.

- Step 5: Repeat these four phrases with prayerful intent to heal this person and your relationship with them. This person could be yourself or even your lingam.

I'm Sorry.
Please Forgive Me.
I Love You.
Thank You.

- Step 6: Imagine that you push a virtual send button to this person while seeing in your mind movie the way you are creating this relationship to be whole and complete going into the future, giving reverence for the lesson of the upset and healing process.

- Step 7: Share your experience with at least three people in the world over the next seven days in person or on social media and what happened as a result of the practice. You will be shocked at the difference you make with people.

Below you will find how I shared this on my Facebook page and how it made a huge difference in my life and the lives of members of my community.

Have you ever disappointed someone you love more than anything in the world?

Have you ever missed a deadline that had you on your knees begging to get the chance back and feeling like nothing can make up for the mistake you made?

It's hard to say I'm sorry.

I messed up.

Please forgive me.

I love you.

Thank you.

These kinds of hard conversations are what I'm out to make easier for people. But that doesn't mean I've got it all handled. Yep, I'm just as scared as the next girl to say I'm sorry.

The other day, I snapped and yelled at my daughter who was cleaning the house so I could have an appointment with a client. I couldn't do the cleaning because of my broken foot.

I was under pressure of time and pain. Not my finest moment. I felt awful and wished I could take it all back. I needed to cool off and so did she. We went to our separate bedrooms to write letters to each other.

After I wrote my letter I reached out to a dear friend and life coach to get some guidance and to see if there was something I missed that if I could put it in would turn the situation around and heal my beloved relationship with my daughter.

His guidance was simple but not easy... admit you messed up. Ask her how she would want to learn how to clean in a way that would work for her. Tell her that she is more important than my to do list. And so I said the hard thing: I'm sorry. Please forgive me. I love you. Thank you. (Ho'oponopono, the Hawaiian forgiveness prayer).

She listened, we read our letters to each other, and we both cried. Then she said what was hard for her to say.... (Courageous vulnerability is like that, if you do it others will feel safe enough to follow.) She told me that the reason she reacted to me the way she did was because she knew I would love her no matter what. She told me that she pushes back with me more than anyone else because I am the safe one who she trusts.

I gave her space and asked her what she needed from me and she said time, understanding, and space. I sat and gave her what she asked for. She cried. I cried. Then she got a blanket and moved closer to me on the couch.

I rescheduled my appointment with the client because she is my priority. We snuggled up with a movie. She reached over and held my hand and all was forgiven.

Did the cleaning go better the next day? Nope. But our relationship and communication did.

I love my girl beyond words. It's hard sometimes to have these conversations with your teenager. But the alternative is more painful.

A family and our community are hurting right now because a young teen took his own life. The fear of all fears of mine. My heart and prayers go out to them and to all who struggle with hard conversations. May we all find our own way to courageous vulnerability that helps us have the hard conversations so we can stay connected with each other.

That's it. The whole practice in a nutshell. Simple and amazingly effective.

As you can see there are many options for saying a gratitude. Your job in this chapter is to notice and see patterns that arise when you have gratitude in your heart or energy field.

Chapter 9

_____

IS THERE A BUG IN MY SOS/SEXUAL OPERATING SYSTEM?

In this chapter we are going to heal, clean up, and clear out past intimacy and relationship wounds. We will use the concept of ROS and SOS and be empowered by what we discovered could create your future you like a phoenix out of the fire of past ups and downs. This is important for the well-being of the individual and partner. The work we do in the chapter meets our need for growth and development aligning with our sixth energy bank at the third eye. I see a future filled with pleasure and delight.

Hard Conversations

About five years ago I was deeply in love with a man who was tall, handsome, had a body to die for, and was a fun creative specialist who worked for a huge game company in San Francisco.

We had met in a transformation course where I was a coach. All of these added up to me being attracted to him.

We loved so many of the same things and seemed to me to be perfect for each other.

I waited the proper six months to strike up a romantic relationship and we started dating. I had a relationship coach who I was being advised by on how to move into these new realms and heal from my divorce. I thought I was doing good and being a star student.

One night we met at a party and went back to my place to have the most amazing intimacy and grew deeper into each other. When we were moving into a lovemaking experience we both clearly wanted each other. We had made love to each other before but it had been awhile, so I thought in the heat of the moment that it was safe for both of us to jump right in. He was so good and responsible making sure we revisit our safe sex talk and choices since we were not exclusively seeing each other yet.

I wanted him so bad and thought he would be so happy to know how bad I wanted him too. I could feel how hard he was and how much he was holding back. As I was encouraging him that I really wanted him and to please take me, I missed his cues that he wanted to go slower and get a condom. I didn't worry as we had reviewed our health sex history and I was fine making love to him without a condom. I trusted him. And I knew that I was clean and clear because I had just been tested with a clean bill of health and I hadn't been intimate with anyone since. There was no need to worry about pregnancy because I was in my early forties with infertility issues for ten years that seemed a sure sign we wouldn't be getting pregnant. Let's ride this ecstasy train baby, and I brought him inside me in one fell swoop. I was oblivious to the assault I had done to this beautiful man. In my naive girl brain, I didn't pay attention to his signs and I essentially raped him.

Days after our sexy night I hadn't heard from him and wondered why he was not reaching out to connect more. One night I worked with my coach and my coach said that I am a masher to men. I honestly didn't know what my coach was talking about. What was a masher? I had never heard this term before so I looked it up. It is a man who attempts to force his unwelcome attentions on a woman.

I was shocked that this was what my coach labeled me as. It wasn't something that I thought I had ever done. I decided to interview my lovers and see if I had been a masher with any of them in the past and started to look into my memories to see if I could remember a time when I had done anything that was like the definition.

And then this experience with Jake, my tall, beautiful, creative sweetheart of a man, came to my awareness. My whole body heated up and became sweaty at the same time. I had done more than masher him; I didn't honor his request to stop and by the time he was inside me his body just took over and released. I was horrified that I could have been so insensitive and irresponsible with another person's personal choices.

All of my training and work on cleaning up my life's messes rushed to the forefront of my mind. I knew what I needed to do, but not one cell in my body wanted to do anything but hide and crawl into a dark hole of shame. I loved this man and I may have lost him for good because of my ignorance and assumption. What was I going to do?

The only thing I could do was call him and clean it up the best I could. Not in order for him to like me, but because if a man had done that to me, I would have wanted him to do the same. This is what I coached my clients to do if they were negatively impacting a relationship. I called him.

When he answered, I got right to it. I told him that I had been thinking of our last time we were together and while I had fond memories about our time together, I realized that I violated his request to not have unprotected sex. I said, "I'm so nervous to talk to you about this. I feel embarrassed that I would have been so disrespectful and forced myself on to you like that. Can you ever forgive me for what I did?"

I shared with him that the relationship coach I worked with referred to me as a masher and that when I looked it up I couldn't believe that described me until I reviewed all my recent experiences and our night together came to my realization along with a hot sweat. I cried and apologized profusely for how my actions must have impacted him.

"You must have a hard time trusting me," I said. "I'm guessing that you don't feel safe to be sexual with me because of what I did."

He was so moved by my apology and touched that I came to understand his experience. He said, "This must have been hard for you to call me about and clean up with me. You are an amazing person and I care much about you. I want to be responsible with my intimacy partners and know that I can trust myself and not just follow my animal desires. I want to save unprotected sex for my committed partner and that was not what I was ready for yet with you. I also don't want an unwanted pregnancy and I can't be sure if I would be able to control myself if I entered you without a condom. I really appreciate how hard of a conversation this must have been for you to have with me. I love you as a friend and want to keep you that way."

My worst fears were confirmed. I had caused him to protect himself from me. What was worse was that I feared he would have this sex wound that would prevent him from being sexually open and vulnerable with others for fear that it would happen to him again.

I told him, "I take full responsibility for what I did. I forced myself on to you and that was essentially rape. I see and feel the impact on you. Please let me know what I can do to clean this up with you. I don't want you to not go out with other women thinking that this will happen again. I know that I have messed up in a big way and have ended my chances to have a romantic relationship with you. That breaks my heart because I love and adore you in a way that I didn't think I would ever find with someone again. That is the impact that I need to resolve with myself. Please know that I want to you have great love and someone to adore you beyond your wildest dreams. I pray that my cleaning this up with you will give you hope for the possibility of a partnership in your future."

Jake was moved by what I had said. "Thank you. You are so amazing, and I wish you the same. Our friendship is more solid because of this conversation. You should be proud of how you handled this difficult situation. It must have been hard for you."

We went on to have an amazing conversation about life and when we would see each other again for a Burning Man gathering with mutual friends. I will never forget the lessons of that day, my mess, and how hard it was to clean it up. It was so hard that I knew going forward in my life I'd rather have the guts to have the hard conversations before I made a mess than have to go back and clean it up afterwards.

Werner Erhard once said in a lecture, "Doing something that is out of integrity in my life at this point is like cutting off one of my fingers. I don't know about you, but I can't afford to cut any more of my digits off. One was bad enough. They don't grow back, you know." I am not willing to cut off any more of my fingers, toes or other body parts. It is painful and you don't get them back. Once integrity is out in a relationship, it is hard work to build it back. It is much easier to put integrity in in the first place.

This was probably not the only time this had happened to Jake. As a matter of fact, since then I have worked with many men about all the times they have been in this kind of situation with woman who thought nothing of taking a man, not knowing that they were violating that man's boundaries.

Whether it is a man or a woman, boundary violation is boundary violation. Just because a man has an erection and gets consumed by the rush of how good it feels to be in a woman, if he didn't want that it is still boundary violating.

I was willing to be the kind of woman who takes responsibility for her mistakes and own the impact on him and on me. I lost the relationship of my dreams in that moment, healed him and cleaned up more than just the wounds I caused. I healed him in that moment of relationship wounds that he didn't even know he had. That is the power of taking responsibility even when it is hard to do so.

We are the walking wounded as human beings. Not one of us gets out of this alive and unscathed. The problem is that the more we are wounded, the more we wound others, and when all those wounds get added up in our lives, we become zombies and behave in a default program ROS that doesn't serve who we really are inside, a sacred being wanting to share love with others.

And like zombies, parts of our bodies are dead and dysfunctional. In this book we learn to heal from life and relationship wounds that have killed our sexual energy. You, as a man, are deeply affected by relationship wounds of betrayal, disrespect, and not being honored. When any of these kinds of wounds have built up in your life what is also being wounded is your heart chakra. I call this your heart castle. If you have enough assault on your heart castle, you will go into protection mode and build a fortress around your heart castle that keeps you from any more damage and assault.

However, this also cuts off the flow of energy to your lingam and soon you will not open and surrender to a woman's love or attention. Jake and I are still good friends, although we don't see each other as often as I would like because we live and work so far from each other. But I know that our breakdown and breakthrough transformed both of our lives and how we handle the autonomy of a sexual partner's safe sex choices. And I learned reverence for a man's body that I don't know if I would have learned if it wasn't for that painful experience.

HARD Conversations Clean-Up Process

This process is a combination of an apology process I've learn from different transformation teachers over the years as well as one I saw work well with students at Supercamp. com. I share this version to support you in your process to make it easy for you. When an apology is necessary, I suggest the Five-Part Apology. This technique allows the person to look beyond the actual incident to consequences and choosing a different behavior, both individuals remain thoughtful and supportive rather than angry or defensive. If you practice this tool with each other, apologies will be easier and more meaningful.

Step 1: Acknowledge

Take responsibility for the breakdown, upset or lack of integrity. Use "I" statements.

Example: "I acknowledge that I changed our plans about dinner without checking in with you, and I only told you at the last minute."

Step 2: Apologize

Acknowledge the cost and impact to others. If unaware of the impact, ask.

Example: "I apologize for not respecting you and for not checking in with you before changing my plans. I know it was hard for you to give up the plans you made with your friends because I needed you to come pick me up."

Step 3: Clean Up the Mess

Deal with the consequences of the breakdown. Ask the person, "Is there anything I can do to clean up the mess with you?" Humbly get their communication without defensiveness. Say thank you. And nothing else other than, "Anything else?" Repeat until they have nothing else to say and then say "Thank you."

Example: "I want to do something to help maintain our relationship. What can I do to clean up the mess?"

Step 4: Reflect on What You Think You Heard Them Say

Once they have stopped telling you how it has impacted them and what would clean it up with them, say the following: "What I think I'm hearing you say is…" (do your best to re-create what they said, not verbatim, just the core essence that is at the heart of their experience of the situation. You don't have to agree with their view, just let them know they have been heard, understood, and valued exactly as they are and exactly as they are not.)

Example: "What I'm hearing you say is that you felt abandoned and not as important as everyone else and that hurt badly because you have a high level need to be significant in my life as my partner."

Step 5: Recommit To Be Count-On-Able

Give your word to the person what they can count on you for going forward. Then do what you said and be who you have committed to being in this area.

Example: "I agree to always respect you and to always check in with you before making any plans that involve you."

Observing the ROS – Relationship Operating System. Part of our hero's journey is to go inside and do core work on self-related to self and self-related to other. This requires having a lens to look at this area of relating that can be the most helpful to get an objective view of how you and your system work or don't work for you and other. When I work with people coaching on relationships, I call it the ROS. For the work I do coaching people on sex and intimacy is the Sexual Operating System or SOS. Looking through the lens of an OS allow us to detach from taking it personally or as a wrong/right conversation. When I studied a lot of Landmark's work sometimes this would be called "What's so" and it's the story or the fiction you have been the author of while pretending it was written by fate and you were a victim to it all along.

Observing the system working/not working gives us another context that empowers us to talk about the what's so without getting tangled in the morass of emotions, shame, blame, guilt and fear, and righteous judgement.

Evaluate what is so. Not what story you say about what is so. If you are not sure how to distinguish what is what happened or fact versus the narration your SOS made up about what happened, sometimes the story can point to the hidden what is so, but it is just the occurring world indicator not what is actually so. A really great book that gets into great detail about unpacking this vicious circle and disempowering cycle is called The Three Laws of Performance. In this book they really helped me to see what's going on with someone by listening to the language they use. Context is decisive and language is always consistent with the person's or company's view of the world. Now this is really big if you can wrap your mind around that part of assessing yours or another's ROS/SOS.

Another component of the OS we will look at to probe new realms of knowing that we don't even know that we don't know is out there is the part of the debugging process of the OS where we send feelers out into the field to ask for guidance from Source, Creator, Universe, Guide, God, or what you use to reference the divine. We assess what you know you know and what you know you don't know to do about the findings. Now this might sound like a bit of double speak, but if you look closely it is an interesting lens to view new realms through as it insists that you look with beginner's eye to see something you never knew existed.

This is a great place to discuss with a coach. Share with the community your findings and what you plan to do about it. When you have someone such as a skilled guide or supportive accountability partner who is supporting you to stay accountable to your commitment to yourself to work through and discover all this, you will move through all of this quicker and smoother than bumping around in the dark. Once you've assessed, observed, gotten curious, and had some aha's about your ROS/SOS, you are going to create a debug. The debug is an interruption in the pattern that isn't working for the purpose of the person's life, relationships, health, sexuality, etc. The debug could be a gentle redirect to have the pattern transmuted to the light side of the program that is running default. It might also look like the OS is fine, but it is clear it is a OS set to default and the other person is so blind to it, so an observer needs to gently, in a safe container, reflect what they see and experience of their OS.

The next step is to test the debug in a safe environment. What I mean by this is to find a relationship to test out your new OS in a container that is safe, respectful, and that you trust. To create that for someone else or for yourself requires integrity, authenticity, responsibility, and being up to something bigger than themselves so the attention is out there with others, instead of fearfully self-obsessing. Run the debug as often as you need. I'm sure you will start to see the ROS/SOS and the bugs faster and faster. When you do start to see patterns so quickly, almost as if it was now an intuition, you will be strengthening the psychic muscle to clean up a mess before it actually is a breakdown in physical form. This process I'm teaching you is a way to hack your own OS's or neurological programing. Once you find your way through the process keep refining. Then rinse and repeat. And live like it is all an experiment, time in the lab of life.

Time for Journaling

When we go deeper into mastery of the hero's journey, you will discover your hidden superpowers. Please do a curiosity journal entry on the following question: What are your habits, patterns, and beliefs? List as many of them as you can. Then, make notes describing what relationship to the OS they have.

What works for you about you/your partner/women/men/family?

What doesn't work about you for you/your partner/women/men/family?

What kind of pattern interrupts do you see or need to stop the spinning of the OS out of control?

Consider: How you do anything is how you do everything. As above so below.

"Regrets are cancer on the soul."
~ Unknown ~

Observe, own, and journal about your pattern of Excuses & Reasons, ways to watch how you make fifty percent integrity masked as 100 percent. Journal about this idea of 100 percent integrity.

To wrap up this chapter and how it applies to ED and the healing that you are here for, the ROS or SOS that runs silently in the background, which makes choices by default and blind, can wreak havoc on the autonomic nervous system that takes direction and suggestions from the OS subconscious. In my experience of healing sexual dysfunction with clients, wounds where they need healing, love, and acceptance for them just the way they are and just the way they aren't. When we have a lack of power, freedom, or self-expression somewhere to look and debug or clean-up is our integrity or authenticity, or getting responsible in an area that you were not originally.

Chapter 10

WHAT JOURNEY IS NEXT
FOR THIS TURNED ON MAN?

In this chapter we explore the seventh step in the *It's HARD* process. This step is connected to the seventh energy bank at the crown of the head where we get our need for spirituality filled and to turning our life's purpose over to being guided by something bigger than you moving up the spiral of enlightenment and sharing with others.

How do we lead the way for others who are going through what you had? Become the next one to pass it on and pay it forward. You will now be creating the Heart-on to Hard-on connection. To have your turn on get stronger and harder you will need to improve your heart's ability to feel emotion and turn upset into excitement.

The conclusion of my work is that ED is an early indication of vascular disease. Heart Dis-Ease. In other words: When a man has had an injury to his heart's desire (energy, dreams, hope, passion, need to create) the spirit of the man's creation lives in his heart. When a man is wounded in this area his survival solution is to build a wall around his heart castle, a fortress. He thinks this will protect him from ever getting hurt again. But actually, it cuts off anything from getting out of the castle as well to the rest of the body, and over time his lingam dies as a result, not the other way around. If I can somehow make this simple to tie it all together.

Our physical body is created by our energy body.

If we have a wound in our energy body that we create protections to survive, that cuts off the flow of energy. Eventually the result is that the physical body without energy flow over long periods of time dies and stops functioning.

To recap: heal wounds, get energy flowing on a regular rhythm, awaken the desire to be excited by a partner, love yourself and your body exactly the way it is and exactly the way it isn't and watch your sleeping giant wake up from its winter's slumber. Celebrate and take him out to play as often as you like.

Once you've done your levels of discovery and practice where your experience has transformed to keep what you've gotten alive for you and contributing in the world you must share it. This brings you into the role of leadership. This doesn't have to be a big song and dance of leadership, but rather a humble, simple template that others can find for themselves as a path to navigate if they are going through something that you went through. This is the next step in mastery, when you take on the role of guide of an apprentice. Even if it is "hey go read this book."

You may be asking yourself, "Now that I have moved through the eye of the needle, how do I keep my stuff working so it isn't hard to climax again?" When in doubt reach out and work the *It's HARD* process. With every practice, you get stronger and stronger, better and better, more and more masterful with ease and grace.

This is where we talk about creating a rich sacred relationship foundation and container for creation to be held. What I have to work with in setting a foundation that is sound enough to support the grandeur of intimate sacred partnership starts with and ends with integrity. This is a word that can confuse many people because most of us collapse integrity into morality. Integrity in the way I have chosen to work with this distinction is about workability or non-workability. Excuses and reasons are ways we make excuses for how we humans make fifty percent integrity masked as 100 percent.

Four Characteristics of a Leader

1. Integrity
2. Authenticity
3. Responsibility/Cause in the matter
4. Being up to something bigger than yourself

I learned this amazing concept of Leadership from the Leadership Course design by Warner Erhard. Leadership is a job for everyone. You will find your own flavor of leadership. When we stand as an example for others to see what is possible in any area of our life we are showing leadership in who we are being. In order to be someone who represents leadership you must educate yourself in communication. I believe that anything can be cleaned up in communication. This is probably obvious, but communication growth and development keep you on course and share what you've learned along the way.

Something important to use in any breakdown is "mess clean up." Now this is not easy for anyone to admit and address with the person that the mess was with. Clean up has an element of humble responsibility. It takes a big person/ leader to take responsibility for a mess and do what it takes to clean it up. HARD Conversations Clean-up Process

Needs are an important filter to check the price of admission for the relationships you find yourself in. The system I have been fine tuning around needs education is set over the template of the chakra or energy center model. If you can feel into the needs that each bank of energy provides to you it will help you put your oxygen mask on first and interrupt the people pleasing pattern.

Well-being is one of the most important themes in all the chapters of this book. Please take care of your well-being. Educate yourself in the area of wellness. Too many people and couples find themselves in a wellness breakdown because they have been stealing from one important aspect of existence to pay another's way. Wellness is truly at the heart of every aspect of your life. Do not wait for the wellness of your life to get out whack. Put workability into the wellness decisions in your relationship.

Finances can also be an area that could break up a couple. This is an expression of energy that can be triggering to people. If we know that this is the case then we can recognize it and transform a trigger into a gold mine.

Life Style Design (LSD) needs to be a topic for discussion early on in any relationship. If your LSD is not a match to my LSD, you will see a couple that struggles. A good example of this could be a couple who have opposite work schedules, so they are always like ships in the night. No sex because the rhythms are completely off.

S.E.X. M.A.G.I.C. is essential for educating yourself and mastering the art of sacred informed intimacy with yourself and others.

Spirituality can be contacted regularly through sexual meditation, guided sensual meditations, and core work that can really only be done by that person. Make this a priority to feed your soul the gift of embodied oneness.

Raul came to see me for an introduction to tantra in a one on one session. He wanted to explore deeper pleasure in his intimacy and relationships, along with ejaculation control.

When I set the container, Raul expressed a real interest in learning what tantra had to offer him and his life. He was a Silicon Valley executive in high tech and worked so much that he didn't really have a lot of time for relationships. However, he had a variety of girlfriends in the locations he traveled to on a regular basis who he cared deeply for and would like to have a deeper connection with.

I started the session with an intro to tantra, breathing, sounding, the ritual, and how we can communicate during the session. He followed my coaching perfectly and danced so beautifully in the ecstasy of the session. After the meditation we went right into all the touches and got him to feel all the parts of his body. As his arousal grew, we moved the energy around and up. He had about three nonejaculatory orgasms before he had a full conscious cum, during which time his speech reverted back to his native tongue of Spanish. He told me later that he went into such a deep state of bliss that when he looked at me, I appeared to him as an angel coming down to adore him. This was when he could only speak to me in Spanish.

I sent him a link with an article to read about incorporating tantra into your life. He is now a regular student.

Raul's text message for me the next day, "Honey… that was an amazing experience… I can't even imagine how a ninety-minute sessions will feel. I really felt someone was taking care of me... I'll keep you updated on how I feel tonight and tomorrow morning. I slept like a baby. I haven't had a good sleep like this in years... Not even when I was in Brazil partying like crazy for four days. One more thing I noticed different, every time I have sex at night the next day I wake up aroused. This time I was peaceful, my mind was quiet, and no thoughts were crossing my mind. I felt kind of complete; there was no worry, no concern, no doubt. The session was one of the most spiritual experiences of my life. Thank you for your caring and dedication."

Whole and complete is a state to keep bringing yourself back to when you feel the attachment to something or an unquenchable desire that you can't stop obsessing about. Upset usually happens when something is incomplete for someone. It is easy to think everything is messed up and too much work to get back to wholeness, which in turn satiates the body.

The whole reason you came to me and my book is because you are not feeling like you are a whole person without your lingam being hard and big when you have the urge for sex. This is what I call a scarcity conversation with yourself.

Journal Entry

What is integrity to you? How can you see that there are times in your relationship where integrity was at the center of something being disempowered? Get curious and connected to see how this goes.

"Man is a goal-seeking animal. His life only has meaning if he is reaching and striving for his goals."

~ Aristotle ~

Chapter 11

PROBLEM SOLVING 101 – GOING FORWARD

As you can see, a lifetime of bumps and bruises on your own hero's journey you didn't ask for is a part of the process. To get this problem with your lingam solved where you can trust your buddy to be hard when you want him to be hard is something you can't put a value on; its priceless to be able to trust your body to do what it's supposed to do. It's the true meaning of manifestation. Our body is the result of our thoughts, feeling, beliefs, and past experiences that are literally dead, no longer happening, not happening now, in the past. In a crazy way we keep thinking that if we just think it through again we'll figure it out this time, and we keep producing the same results in our lives, thinking we should have made something new happen.

This process is long and hard to do on your own. I did all my healing work with a coach and the support of programs like mine to keep me on track and accountable to partners to get through the really hard times when I wanted to give up and do what felt easy in just going back to the past.

We are here on earth school together for a reason, otherwise we would all be put on islands for solo work. Relationships are where the rubber meets the road and you apply in real time the new skills you are developing. Don't do this by yourself. Ask for help from someone. If I'm not the person you feel comfortable with then find someone who you do feel comfortable with.

But beware of a pitfall that I see catch a lot of people. The feeling of comfort is actually a decoy. The work we do together is not going to feel comfortable. It feels awful to go into the rooms of your heart castle that you boarded up years ago because your high school sweetheart kissed a guy in a game of Truth or Dare. But on the other side of that dark room with cobwebs and painful images and stories of her betrayal is your lingam's virility and juicy functioning erection. You will be a teenager again once you've swept the castle clean of all that past that is getting in the way of loving openly and freely.

"Fifty-seven percent of men who have bypass surgery had prior ED. Sixty-five percent of men hospitalized for myocardial infarction experienced prior ED. The majority of ED is linked to vascular disease. ED could be an indicator of systemic atherosclerosis or an early warning for myocardial infarction or stroke."

~ Dr. Ted Jablonski ~

The well-being side of your erectile function is just as important as all of the spiritual, emotional, and psychological sides of your problem. In this chapter I'm going to go over a wide array of things you can do to improve your well-being to aid in strengthening your erection and sexual functionality.

There are many ways to improve your well-being to support your sexual function. I've made a list below that will help you search to learn more. Anyone of these would be the topic of another book. I encourage you to participate in my support groups and programs to help you navigate your way through all the extra things that can be done to improve your health. When in doubt follow nature's way of life and growth and you can't go wrong. Oxygen, water, detox regularly, and find activities that increase these in your body.

- Prostate Massage
- GAINSWave Therapy
- Peptide Supplementation
- Cold Water Hydro Therapy
- Essential Oils Natures Medicine Cabinet
- Neuroscience of Tantra and Ancient Healing Modalities
- Homeopathy
- Osteopathy
- Exercise
- Detoxification from Environmental Toxins and/or Medications
- Nutrition and food as medicine
- Meditation
- Guided Visualizing, Hypnosis or Neuro-linguistic Programming
- Oxygen Therapy
- Restorative Health

Chapter 12

YOU'VE DONE IT.
JUST KEEP GETTING BACK UP.

You made it to your beacon that you set at the very beginning of the book. We have traveled from your experience of hard to climax and frustration all the way out to dancing in the mystical cosmos of ecstasy and back to earth. You have experienced full body orgasm in yourself and hopefully started sharing this juicy pleasure with a partner. And your wand of light has new life and vitality.

From the very beginning of this book's creation I've wanted this book to be filled with the lesson of epic forgiveness, epic love, and epic sex. As I created this book my intention was for you to receive this as my love letter to you, the representative of the divine masculine. I revere you in all the forms you come in. My wish for you, my dear man, is that you experience divine love from the feminine. We love you and want you to love the life you have.

I know the world has its way of knocking you down, but no matter how many times it knocks you down I pray that you get back up. Just keep getting back up. And if ever you need support, it is the strong grounded man who asks for support, especially from his partner. Build trust with them. Show this person what strength and courage it takes to be vulnerable. You will be surprised how much of a turn-on it is to have your man need you.

Remember, before you do anything ground yourself. Practice this grounding every day and you will be surprised how this alone will bring back the strength of your lingam's erection. We are human beings and spirit. We need to be connected to the earth's energy field and the universe's energy field because we are a hybrid of these to magical forces.

Get present, it's a gift beyond measure to be in the moment. Don't sell out this gift to the past or the future. If you combine this with being grounded there is almost nothing you can't do. This is what the martial arts masters do to be ready for anything.

Stay in your body. If an experience is too intense, pause, eye gaze something around the room to stay in the moment, and breathe slowly to fully embody who you are in this moment. Breath deep and slow. Oxygen is the most important element for healing everything. When in doubt, get your circulation and oxygen to increase from anything from yogic breathing during love making, to cold showers that increase capillaries' expansion, to exercise. Find ways to get your body as healthy as possible. Your erectile virility is directly correlated to your relaxation and well-being of mind, body, and spirit.

Communicate and show reverence for your partner. Have a gratitude practice every day where you practice creating appreciation and acknowledgements of anything and everything. When we can see the beauty in anything is when we are truly free from suffering. Make sure to acknowledge the people in your life. You will be amazed by how much people will want to acknowledge you when you give appreciation to them. There is something that can be acknowledged in everyone, even that person you are thinking right now would be impossible. Find something and have reverence for the fact that that person is doing the best they can at that very moment.

Practice asking for want you want while in sexy time. Do this with someone you trust so you can get better without the fear of doing it wrong. Be ok with a no or a yes. Know that you are the only one who can know what your needs are and get them filled. Getting your needs filled by another person is one of the beautiful benefits of tantra yoga lovemaking. When you lay with your partner all your chakras are aligned and your energies are woven with your partner's, which is meeting both of your needs all seven all at once by making energetic love to the divine you see in your partner.

Exercise forgiveness and make it a practice for you to be free of regret and frustration. If you are having a hard time letting go of something, get support. The wounds of days past is the quickest way to kill off any arousal in your body. Love and gratitude increase energy and bring life.

Get creative. You are here to create. That is what the sexual energy is best at, creating, so have fun with it. Liberate your creative juices and spread the abundance. The law of abundance is the more you create and share the more it grows and spills over into all areas of your life. Creation is simple and very youthful. Bring back your inner teenager. If not now, when would be a good time to live full out?

ACKNOWLEDGMENTS

This book was written on the backs of many men I love and have loved all my life. To you all, I bow in the deepest of gratitude, love, honor, and respect. I know I, as a woman/girl/lady in your life, have made mistakes for at the time I knew not what I was doing and for all of those known and unknown mistakes I have made, I humbly apologize for the impact on your life.

My wish is that this book heals the impact of my mistakes by taking what I've learned from my mistakes and heal the wounds in all of humanity, gender identity aside. I'm doing this work because I believe in us as loving humans to rise to a new sacred partnership of the divine masculine & feminine. May the generations that are birthed from our new age continue to grow and create more and more awake conscious beings of light and love.

I write this book so that I never forget that every man was once some mother's baby boy. In honor of the three baby boys that died in my womb, who I never got to raise, this book is my love letter that I would have left you – to teach you how to be good men and lovers. To Alden, Lorenzo, Everett and your sisters, Coco Rose and Sydaleelee, thank you for teaching me what love is.

This book is dedicated to my grandpa Stafford, grand-daddy Dowden, my hero and father Tony, my brother Kiss, my godfathers Kent and Ed, and my uncles John, Bruce, Richard. To my cousins: Johnny, Jimmy, Mark, Greg, Brian, William, Guy, Dean, Daniel, Wayne, and Anthony. To my former husband, Dan, my brother-in-law's, and my high school sweetheart, Wally. To my college sweethearts Andrew and Matt. To the women and men who believed in me so much that you supported me writing this book: Mom and Dad, Auntie Gloria, Julie, Gina U., John Rozenberg, Matt Klee, Josh J., Craig, Erik B., Doron, John K., Andy, Brad, Chris, Scott, Jerry, Danny. To my teachers: Warner Erhart and Landmark Leaders, Source School of Tantra's Charles and Christy Muir, Caroline Muir, TJ Bartel, Leah Piper, Hank Wesselman, Erwan and Alica Davon, Rhys Thomas, Lisa Campion, Cindy Toone, all the men who have loved me and that I have loved in my life, my clients and most of all to the man who will someday love and cherish my beloved daughter, and all the women who love or have loved these men and boys.

A very special, deep-dive thank you to Dr. Angela Lauria, Cheyenne Giesecke, Ramses Rodriguez, my editors Ora North, Todd Hunter, Cory Hott, and the entire Author Incubator team. You were the wind beneath my wings from panic to product, complete and all the more. Only you know what it took to have me be the author who made the difference this book makes in the world.

May this book guide you to your own personal heart castle held in the arms of your beloved. May you find the great love you've always wanted but didn't know how to find and the woman or man or person to cherish you exactly the way you are and exactly the way you aren't. I love you. I'm sorry. Please forgive me for I know not what I do. Thank you!

THANK YOU

———————

Thank you for reading my book and taking this journey with me all the way through the eye of the needle. I love each and every one of you for your commitment, hard work, and belief in me to deliver a way to bliss beyond your wildest dreams. You are the sacred chivalry leaders of the future.

As a thank you, I've created a video series of exercises, talks, and meditations that will support your new S.E.X. practice going to the next level. Your secret thank you gift is ready for you at www.ItsHardBook.com/thx.

I'm passionate about helping others with sexual healing and dysfunction. Please keep in touch (I'm active on Facebook, Instagram, and Twitter – tag me at @S.Sequoia.Stafford and use the hashtag #ItsHard), and feel free to touch others by sharing how this work made a difference in your life. You would be amazed by how many people I've had amazing conversations with about this book and its topic. Everyone is dying to have someone to talk to about hard topics. Be that person or refer them to me and my new podcast, Hard Conversations with Sequoia.

Blessings, light, and love,
Sequoia

ABOUT THE AUTHOR

S. SEQUOIA STAFFORD is an author, speaker, master healer, recovering perfectionist, and compulsive hard worker. She has combined over twenty years of transformational studies and practices in order to create the It's Hard process, a unique healing modality for modern sexual well-being.

Her path to wholeness and personal health resulted a love of life that gets her up in the morning. Along the way, she trained with masters in the fields of shamanism, tantra, psychological gestalt theory, sacred sexuality, hypnosis, mysticism and full-spectrum energy medicine.

She is tenacious and chooses to have her hard work be a labor of love and healing of sexual dysfunction for anyone. Working in the entertainment industry since she was fifteen – first as a fashion and spokes model, then as an actress, director, teacher and producer – she saw firsthand the ontological ways humans use sexual energy to create or destroy. She is so grateful for finding the healing art of tantric yoga to bring wellness to herself and clients – all of which led to the culmination of her life dream to heal, perform, create, and love.

Sequoia's discovery of the science of now guides seekers to be the healthiest human beings possible, from anywhere they find themselves on the journey. She helps clients discover their bliss through guided self-growth and development practices designed specifically for them and what they are dealing with in life. She proudly helps people spend less time in the therapist's office and more time in the bedroom.

DIFFERENCE
P R E S S

ABOUT DIFFERENCE PRESS

Difference Press is the exclusive publishing arm of The Author Incubator, an educational company for entrepreneurs – including life coaches, healers, consultants, and community leaders – looking for a comprehensive solution to get their books written, published, and promoted. Its founder, Dr. Angela Lauria, has been bringing to life the literary ventures of hundreds of authors-in-transformation since 1994.

A boutique-style self-publishing service for clients of The Author Incubator, Difference Press boasts a fair and easy-to-understand profit structure, low-priced author copies, and author-friendly contract terms. Most importantly, all of our #incubatedauthors maintain ownership of their copyright at all times.

Let's Start a Movement with Your Message

In a market where hundreds of thousands of books are published every year and are never heard from again, The Author Incubator is different. Not only do all Difference Press books reach Amazon bestseller status, but all of our authors are actively changing lives and making a difference.

Since launching in 2013, we've served over 500 authors who came to us with an idea for a book and were able to write it and get it self-published in less than 6 months. In addition, more than 100 of those books were picked up by traditional publishers and are now available in book stores. We do this by selecting the highest quality and highest potential applicants for our future programs.

Our program doesn't only teach you how to write a book – our team of coaches, developmental editors, copy editors, art directors, and marketing experts incubate you from having a book idea to being a published, bestselling author, ensuring that the book you create can actually make a difference in the world. Then we give you the training you need to use your book to make the difference in the world, or to create a business out of serving your readers.

Are You Ready to Make a Difference?

You've seen other people make a difference with a book. Now it's your turn. If you are ready to stop watching and start taking massive action, go to http://theauthorincubator.com/apply/.

"Yes, I'm ready!"

OTHER BOOKS BY DIFFERENCE PRESS

Am I the Reason I'm Not Getting Pregnant?: The Fearlessly Fertile Method for Clearing the Blocks between You and Your Baby by Roseanne Austin

Career or Fibromyalgia, Do I Have To Choose?: The Practical Approach to Managing Symptoms and the Life You Love by Karen R. Brinklow

Damsel No More!: The Secret to Slaying Your Anxiety and Loving Again after an Abusive Relationship by Emily Davis

Help! My Husband Is Hardly Home: 8 Steps to Feel Supported While Raising Your Family by Kelsey Domiana

The Divorced Mom Makeover: Rise Up, Reclaim Your Life, and Rock On with Your Gorgeous Self by Jamie Hernandez, M.A.

The Right Franchise for You: Escape the 9 to 5, Generate Wealth, & Live Life on Your Terms by Faizun Kamal

Overcome Thyroid Symptoms & Love Your Life: The Personal Guide to Renewal & Re-Calibration by Vannette Keast

The Luminary Journey: Lessons from a Volcano in Creating a Healing Center and Becoming the Leader You Were Born to Be by Darshan Mendoza

The End Is Near: Planning the Life You Want after the Kids Are Gone by Amie Eyre Newhouse

When Marriage Needs an Answer: The Decision to Fix Your Struggling Marriage or Leave Without Regret by Sharon Pope

Leadership through Trust & Collaboration: Practical Tools for Today's Results-Driven Leader by Jill Ratliff

Conquer Foot Pain: The Art of Eliminating Pain by Improving Posture so You Can Exercise Again by Julie Renae Smith, MPT

The Art of Connected Leadership: The Manager's Guide for Keeping Rock Stars and Building Powerhouse Teams by Lyndsay K.R. Toensing

Financial Freedom for Six-Figure Entrepreneurs: Lower Taxes, Build Wealth, Create Your Best Life by Jennifer Vavricka

BAD (Begin Again Differently): 7 Smart Processes to Win Again after Suffering a Business Loss by Claudette Yarbrough